D1498997

A FIGHT TO FORGIVE

HOW TO TURN THEIR WRONGS AND YOUR HURTS INTO GOD'S GREATER PURPOSES

KEVIN RAMSBY

A FIGHT TO FORGIVE

Copyright © 2016 by Kevin Ramsby. All rights reserved. No part of this publication may be reproduced, stored in a retrieval system, or transmitted in any form or by any means—electronic, mechanical, photocopy, recording, or any other—except for brief quotations in printed reviews, without the prior permission of Kevin Ramsby. Requests may be submitted by email: kevinramsby@yahoo.com

All Scripture verses, unless otherwise indicated, are taken from the Holy Bible, New International Version®, NIV® Copyright © 1973, 1978, 1984, 2011 by Biblica, Inc.® Used by permission. All rights reserved worldwide.

Scripture quotations marked "KJV" are taken from the King James Version. Public domain. http://www.BibleGateway.com

Scripture quotations marked "NLT" are taken from the Holy Bible, New Living Translation, copyright © 1996, 2004, 2007 by Tyndale House Foundation. Used by permission of Tyndale House Publishers, Inc., Carol Stream, Illinois 60188. All rights reserved.

Editorial services by Maureen Tisdale Batty. LiveLoveEdit.com

Self-publishing counsel and strategy provided by Servus Publishing. ServusPublishing.com

Cover Photo: Viktor Gladkov/Shutterstock

*To my beautiful wife, Sarah, and awesome kids, Noah and Caitlin.
Thank you for lovingly encouraging me and sacrificing so much
in being supportive of the Lord's unique purposes in my life:
serving the people and inner city of Detroit.*

TABLE OF CONTENTS

PASTOR TIM DILENA

We don't have many heroes today. We have celebrities, but not many heroes. Typically, celebrities aren't known because of their character, but because of their exposure—they are celebrated because they have been on TV or gone viral. Heroes, on the other hand, are known for character, and that's very different from celebrity. Character has a journey to it, a journey of pain and making it to the other side.

Kevin is such a hero, and *A Fight to Forgive* is such a journey— full of facing unknowns, twists, and eventually the lessons of healing, forgiveness, and purpose that God had to teach Kevin in the wake of what happened on August 4, 2009.

As Kevin's pastor, boss, neighbor, and friend, I had box seats for the beginning of the journey.

"Pastor, do you think this is real?" I remember hearing those words over the phone from Kevin's wife Sarah at 3:30 a.m. in my hotel room in Minneapolis. Sarah had just received a phone call from Henry Ford Hospital, telling her that Kevin had had an accident and was going into surgery. She and I had no idea what "accident" meant, nor of the magnitude of what had happened at that time.

We hardly could have guessed Kevin had been stabbed 37 times.

Two hours later, I was on a 5:30 a.m. flight back to Detroit. It was the longest hour-and-a-half flight I have ever taken, followed by unforgettable days and nights dealing with the unimaginable. Nothing prepares you for something like this. I'll never forget carefully choosing how much information to get to Sarah before she got to the hospital, praying and waiting with family and friends there, or hearing the surgeon say, "Kevin will live, but he has a long road of recovery ahead of him." The word "live" was all that was needed for this journey to begin, though it had many more miles to go from there.

Kevin's story needs to be told. Why? Because bad stuff happens to people? No. That's just a fact; bad things happen all the time. But those who see catastrophe through for the good to come out of it, that's a select group, and Kevin Ramsby is in it. Good wasn't all that came out of Kevin being alive despite 37 stab wounds, gold came out of it.

This book shares that gold.

Many, many years ago, an old church mother looked at me one night and said "Pastor, no test, no testimony." I've never forgotten that, and Kevin is a perfect example.

The attack was Kevin's test.

This book is Kevin's testimony.

—Pastor Tim Dilena,
Our Savior's Church (Lafayette, Louisiana)

FOREWORD

JIM COCKRUM

Imagine, for a moment, a senseless, meaningless, brutal crime being committed in one of the most heartless, evil ways you can imagine. Now imagine that the victim is one of the most giving and caring people you've known and loved for more than two decades.

I'm sorry to get so raw so fast, but that's the ride you are in for as you turn these pages.

That said, *A Fight to Forgive* isn't about how great of a person Kevin Ramsby is (though he is one of the best men I know), or about the depths of evil that can be stored up in the human heart. Instead, this book is about something far more challenging to the soul.

Forgiveness.

I had two emotions when my wife Andrea and I got the call from Kevin's wife Sarah letting us know he had been attacked: concern for the Ramsbys and hatred for whoever did this. Forgiveness? Oh, please. I wanted a fight, some justice, and a conviction, or at least a nice dose of Hollywood-style vengeance. And I wasn't alone. To attack this caring man who spends his days helping underserved families was a surefire way to draw the anger of the thousands he has served in Detroit for decades.

But the thing is, Pastor Kevin *himself* forgave the man who attacked him. By doing so, and sharing where and how he found the strength and guidance for such an impossible journey, he brought along those of us who love him most, making our own journey to forgiveness simple in comparison.

Now, it's your turn. If you've been wronged or hurt by someone and you haven't yet forgiven the offender, your life story is in dire jeopardy. Unforgiveness will rot a person to their core, and if that's true for you, you desperately *need* the message contained in this simple, honest book. Kevin has shown us a way to do the seemingly impossible. He has our battle plan.

So insert yourself into these pages. The events and details that you are about to read are as true as they are unbelievable—brutal evil happened, and having walked closely with Kevin in the years since the attack, I can attest that the pain still lingers in many ways. But *forgiveness* has been the key to unlocking beautiful doors that no other force of nature could have ever opened in his life, in mine, and in those of others who've known him personally.

May your soul find the strength required to step into the ring and do battle with pure evil, and then having done battle, exit the ring stronger than before the bell rang.

God bless you, reader—the fight starts now.

—Jim Cockrum
Author and Bible-Based Business/Life Coach

PREFACE

Twenty-eight years ago, I was a teenager consumed with only three things: me, me, and me. My life goal was to make a lot of money while doing the least amount of work and, of course, partying. God was not even a blip on my radar. I had no desire for and little knowledge of Christianity.

Through several experiences—coming home bloodied after a fist fight, nearly being expelled from the entire school district for making a bomb threat, and my mom being diagnosed with cancer—I came to see that my life was not headed in a good direction. Wanting to stay out of trouble, I began attending a church youth group where I heard that God, through Jesus Christ, desired to have a personal relationship with *me*, despite everything.

My life made a 180-degree turn one night when I committed not to a religion, but to that relationship with Jesus who was sent by God the Father to die an unjust death for my past, present, and future sins. For the first time, I was freed from the shame and guilt I carried; I felt like I was a brand new person. As my priorities shifted from me, me, and me to God, others and *then* me, I turned away from pursuing an accounting degree to attend North Central Bible College and be trained in ministry.

My incredible youth pastor, Jeanne Mayo, taught me true faith is choosing to trust the character of God even when outward circumstances are impossible to understand. So instead of going out with everyone on weekends, I often spent hours alone in a prayer room seeking knowledge of God's character. I'd also seek God's purposes for my life, and I began to follow His leadings no matter how they looked on paper. For example, I turned down the best internship in youth ministry when I heard about the needs found in the inner cities of America and felt God led me to pursue ministry there instead. I went on to live my life guided by faith in a God I could not see, but could most definitely trust.

But then, that was all before the attack.

On August 4, 2009, I was stabbed 37 times in my own home in Highland Park, Michigan, by a crazed intruder high on cocaine. As I lay bleeding to death with my intestines on the cold tile next to me, I couldn't imagine anything positive—let alone great—could come out of the life-shattering attack. Little did I know the importance of the lessons God could teach me, or how badly those lessons are needed by so many others. Hurting people are everywhere, and that includes my attacker, whose real name will not appear in this book to avoid heaping unnecessary shame or guilt upon him for actions he regrets.

As I set out to put my journey into words, I quickly found a hero in the Old Testament's Joseph. Talk about someone who knew a little something about wrongs and hurts being allowed into his life— after his brothers became jealous of dreams he had of being in a position of power, they threw him in a pit and sold him into slavery. And that was only the beginning of the ongoing waves of hurt and wounds his brothers set in motion: Joseph lost years with his beloved dad, was sent to prison for a crime he didn't commit, and got forgotten by those who made promises to help.

Despite all that, Joseph made room for God to turn things around. Decades later, Joseph revisited his painful past, and what he said to his wrongdoers then became the guiding verse for my journey in the wake of the attack:

> You intended to harm me, but God intended it for good to accomplish what is now being done, the saving of many lives. (Genesis 50:20)

Joseph's eventual response to the hellish fallout of his brothers' actions—that it's possible to become matter-of-fact about a painful past and focus on a beautiful future—is simply amazing. How can someone who was so wronged invite the very people responsible up close to him, and then be willing to serve them? How is it even possible to forgive when years of life have been affected and dreams have been crushed? What role does God play in our lives in response to the unjust and hurtful actions of others?

It is the purpose of this book to address those questions specifically. I've discovered, through both my own journey and studying Joseph and other Biblical stories and truths, that making room for God to turn others' wrongs and our hurts into His greater good involves:

- revealing the wrongs by sharing what happened (this may be telling a trusted person, the offender, or even the Lord);

- acknowledging the hurts that came out of it;

- coming to trust God after He allows wrongs and hurt;

- fighting opponents and obstacles like fear and bitterness to eventually reframe the story from the point of view of a victor, not a victim;

- and ultimately discovering God's purposes in and for our lives.

See, as powerful as forgiveness is, being able to discover God's purposes in our lives really is the ultimate prize here, the triumph that truly makes all the work worth it. After all, who doesn't long to know what God wants to do in and through us?

My hope in sharing with you three things—what God has taught me in the wake of the attack; the practical, specific ways I applied those lessons; and the gifts that have come from doing so—is that you too can enjoy a Genesis 50:20 triumph.

But you know, Genesis 50:20 is the end of the story. Remember, the dream God gave Joseph earlier in his story became a nightmare before the intended good showed up.

That's true of my story too.

OPENING SCENE

"I CAN'T BELIEVE THIS IS HAPPENING"

He is dragging my bleeding body along my floor. In my house. The hardwood floor my wife Sarah and I had painstakingly stripped, stained, and varnished.

Gripping my right hand, which had already been decimated by his knife blade, he hauls me toward the kitchen as I gasp for air through waves of excruciating pain.

I can't believe this is happening to me, I think, not for the first time. It's too surreal; I'm usually greeted affectionately here by the door, not stabbed, grabbed, and dragged.

Now I'm dropped flat on my face as my attacker lets go of my hand. Face down, I'm sure I'm paralyzed from his most recent stabs—six or seven thrusts to the base of my neck, some so deep a finger can fit in them. Electrical-type twinges shoot throughout my body.

He wants my car keys, and I'd told him where I put them, in the kitchen. He heads in to rummage for them there, in the same room where just hours before I'd call my friend Peter about how to cook tenderloin.

As he heads into the kitchen, my mind wanders to my two kids. Noah, my pride and joy, is a sports-loving twelve-year-old I love to coach. Caitlin, just a month shy of nine, is all into the dress-up dolly princess thing, and she has me wrapped around her finger, as my wife would say.

Lying bleeding to death where my children usually burst through the door asking "What's up?" I desperately want to see them again, to throw the football with Noah or hear Caitlin call me Daddio on our weekly breakfast date to Coney Island.

I have to do something. I must get out of this situation. *No one is a violent home intruder every moment of his life. Maybe he has kids.* I try to lift my head to see where he is, but I can't. So I aim my voice toward the kitchen.

"I have two incredible kids," I call out between gasps for air. "Please take whatever you want and just leave. I have two kids, please, *please* just take everything and go. I have *kids!*"

I hear him stop what he is doing and a moment later, his footsteps as he approaches me. Maybe this is it: that moment, like in the movies, where the criminal shows his humanity. Perhaps he'll say something now, something other than "Where are the keys and where is the money?"

He does not.

Instead, he wordlessly resumes stabbing me.

That's when I know hopelessness at a deeper level than ever before, or ever since.

My attacker won't stop.

I can't stop him.

And God isn't stopping him.

PART ONE

REVEALING THE WRONGS

THE ATTACK

CHAPTER 1

LIVING THE DREAM

"I'll call you later," Sarah says.

"Whatever," I respond under my breath.

I'd just come home from picking up a family heirloom to find my wife packing for her last-minute trip to hang out with our kids at her parents' house. I'd been thinking we'd spend some time together before she left, but Sarah, exhausted from a particularly busy week of ministry, is preoccupied with the seven-hour drive ahead of her.

I guess she doesn't care we won't see each other for a week, I think, walking back up the pathway to our house as Sarah drives off.

Oh well, I think. It's been a busy two weeks; now, it's time to start knocking out some of these annoying household tasks I desperately need to tackle here at 110 Montana Street.[i] And maybe, to pull back from the chilly moment with Sarah and think about the big picture.

The truth is on August 3, 2009, I have a great life. I've been married to my beautiful wife for 14 years, have two awesome kids and am a pastor at a church I've loved and served for five years. Life seems so perfect; God has placed us in a community we absolutely love, and our

---

[i]   Address changed to protect privacy.

family is thriving. In the nine months we've lived here, I've grown to love the small-town feel of our tight-knit neighborhood; we look out for and visit one another, have cook-outs and help each other in any way possible. We love to play kickball in the street with the family of Tim Dilena, our head pastor who lives right around the corner, and we play catch in the backyard.

I'd better start with the yard. It's starting to resemble the overgrown one of the abandoned home four doors down, since I haven't touched it for days due to War Week. That outreach— when high school students from around the country crash at the church to help with community projects in between powerful and life-changing services—is basically church camp on steroids, and I absolutely love it. I can practically feel the energy of those kids still vibrating through the community as I push the lawnmower around our small yard.

Before I know it, the yard and house are back in order, or at least reasonably so. It's unusually quiet with just me and my dog, Maggie; regardless, it's home. We worked and saved for it most of our decade-plus living and pastoring in Detroit, then for more than a year we labored tirelessly to turn a typical vacant house in one of the most violent and desolated cities in America into our sanctuary.

Living in an area where so many vacant houses are targeted by squatters and scrappers, we tend to leave the right lights on and keep a big dog in the house. But while I take such precautions, I don't live in fear. This is where the Lord led my family to live, and it is easy to relax into trusting that He has angels watching over us. So toward the end of the day, when I light the bright chandelier at the foot of the stairwell to let outsiders know our home is occupied, I don't give a thought to whether I'm safe. I simply assume I am, and head upstairs.

Ready to chill in our room on the second floor, I flip on *The King of Queens* and settle down with my laptop. It feels great to finally jump into bed after working all day around the house. I'm still thinking about the incredible week of outreach. Hundreds of kids signed up for a new citywide kids sports program I'd wanted to do for years, so my fingers begin typing as fast as possible to input data from the sign-up cards.

In addition to being pumped about War Week, I'm excited about the upcoming week; in just two short days, I'm to fly with Pastor Tim to Oklahoma City for a conference to prepare for heading up a Revival Tabernacle church plant in a few months. Having recently sold my business renting inflatables for parties to focus on ministry, I am ecstatic about living on purpose: loving God, loving people, and serving both in the heart of Detroit.

Can this be my life? Are all my dreams really coming true?

Okay, I'm sweating to death in this room. It feels like an oven, I think, getting up to blast the air conditioner as cold as possible on this hot, muggy August night.

So when I finally push the computer aside around midnight, I fall asleep with the TV blaring and the window AC unit blowing hard and loud. It isn't exactly quiet, but it is peaceful, for a 37-year-old pastor loving life and trusting in the Lord.

Of course, I have no clue about the devastation that is coming in just three short hours.

CHAPTER 2
THE SHATTERING GLASS

SMASH crash scatter scatter scatter.

I jump to my feet, heart pounding.

What was THAT?

I instantly sprint toward the stairwell. I'm about to hit the first step when I remember my wallet is easily accessible on my bedroom dresser, so I run back in and throw it across the room. Turning back to the stairs, I race toward the sound of the shattering glass.

It doesn't occur to me to hide or call the police. My nickname in high school was Rambo; when I face a threat, my instinct is to run toward it, not from it.

I grab the first thing I see that I could swing at somebody, a tennis racket. Racing down the stairs toward the landing, I bang the racket against the walls as hard as I can, shouting "THIS IS MY HOUSE! GET OUT! THIS IS MY HOUSE!" My blood is rushing as fast as I am. It's not just some property that's in jeopardy here: this is my dream home, the place where I staked a claim in a city I love with a family I love. It's *not* to be messed with.

When I hit the landing, I pivot back toward the second floor, yelling, "QUICK, GO GET THE GUN, GET THE GUN!" There is no gun, much less anyone to get it, but I hope the threat of one will change any potential intruder's mind.

Turning back around, I continue hollering "THIS IS MY HOUSE! THIS IS MY HOUSE! GET OUT!" in an unfamiliar, adrenaline-laced voice as I race down the second half of the flight of stairs. I've armed myself the best I can with the only thing I have, and that tennis racket is raised and ready for action as I charge toward what's coming.

That racket is later found in a pool of my blood with a knife cut through the cover.

Everything will go wrong this night.

Everything.

CHAPTER 3

FIGHTING FOR MY LIFE

It is on the final two steps of my winding stairwell that I see him.

I have no idea who he is, only that he doesn't belong in my house. Muscular and shirtless, he seems huge. Barreling around the corner toward me, he doesn't say a word as I'm hollering "THIS IS MY HOUSE!" and launching myself off the stairs at him, tennis racket reared back.

I am in mid-air when I catch a glimpse of the large butcher knife he is holding, and all I can do is try to knock it out of his hand with the strongest swing of the tennis racket I can muster.

I fail.

So I let go of the racket to try to tackle him. As I say one last time "THIS IS MY HOUSE!" my attacker thrusts the knife at me while I hurl myself at him.

He does not fail.

The knife plunges deep into my abdomen. My leap comes to an abrupt halt, my hands clenching my attacker's broad, bare shoulders.

With the knife inside me piercing my colon and small intestine, life seems to pause.

For a split second, my attacker and I make eye contact underneath that well-lit chandelier that was supposed to be a safety precaution. His eyes—something's not right with his eyes. They're bugging out, intense, wild, yet with a coldness, an absence of emotion. It's an image instantly and permanently burned into my consciousness, and my thoughts turn.

I'm not going to see tomorrow.

Breathing hard, blood still boiling in battle mode, I begin throwing punches at the intruder in the brightly lit entranceway of my home. He doesn't say a thing; he just pulls the knife from my abdomen and begins thrusting it back into me over and over.

I do everything possible to try to block each aggressive swing, but it's quickly apparent there is nothing I can do to subdue him; he is like a pit bull locked onto his prey, not letting go until victory. His actions don't seem like those of a simple thief. There's darkness and evil intent, a wild desperation and determination unlike anything I've seen before.

I can't believe this is happening. I can't believe this is going to be my last night.

Almost immediately, my hands go from punching to trying to protect myself from the overwhelming knife blows. With a seven- inch gash in my abdomen, I'm not standing for long. When I fall to my hands and knees, he jumps on me and I collapse, landing on my back right in front of my entryway door. I'm no longer fighting; I'm no longer able to.

Even with me on the floor, the guy doesn't stop; he straddles me and continues to stab me over and over and over. He just misses my eye, but gets me in the temple. Three, maybe four stabs to the chest, one barely missing my heart. The front door that could lead to outside help is just feet away, but it's of no use to me. I'm completely pinned under a knife-wielding attacker who is strung out on crack cocaine, possessed with getting money for his next hit, and wildly stabbing at me.

Never in my wildest imagination would I have thought my path as a pastor—one who has dedicated his life to working in the heart of Detroit under God's direction and care—might end with an obituary that reads "murdered and stabbed to death in the safety of his home."

This isn't supposed to happen to me.

CHAPTER 4

THE FIGHT KNOCKED OUT OF ME

I can't believe this is happening to me.

While my mind wanders in and out of disbelief, my attacker continues to slash the knife down at me, getting me numerous times in the upper chest and face. Aware that winning the fight by being the last man standing isn't possible at this point, I switch my goal to something simpler: survival.

So I try to shake my attacker off by thrashing back and forth beneath him. It doesn't work and while I try, he lands two stabs to the throat. I'm able to partially block those so they don't go all the way through. I'm not so lucky with another stab, which penetrates my cheek and goes into my mouth.

Meanwhile, in between enduring defensive wounds on my forearms as I try to deflect and block stabs, I am trying to grab hold of his hand and get the knife. In that effort, I catch one of the stabs in between my pinkie and ring finger on my left hand, severely damaging the nerves and tendons. I feel none of this; everything in me is just screaming, "I WANT TO LIVE!" more and more desperately as the seconds, which seem like an eternity, tick by.

Then, all of a sudden, a ray of light.

The knife is in my hand.

Wait—what?

The knife is in my hand!

I can't believe it. How exactly could it have transferred from his hand to mine? No matter—I have something with which to defend myself at last. More importantly, I have hope. Maybe I can get out of here—maybe I can live after all!

So the second I catch the knife, I yank it away from him and begin trying to stab upward as fast and hard as I can, fueled by this surprise surge of hope. I nick him a few times, though he stays on top of me, scrambling to get the weapon back.

This, it turns out, is actually the least of my problems.

What I'm clenching so tightly in my desperation to gain the upper hand is the knife's blade, not its handle. So each time I stab, the sharp steel tears through the nerves and tendons of my thumb, which is already damaged from me catching the knife during a downward stab.

What is supposed to be a game-changer turns into yet another devastating injury. Then, after a few attempts at defending myself, I feel the blade, slick from my own blood, slip from my grip. I lose sight of the weapon, never to get hold of it again. It hits the floor, along with any hope about gaining control of this situation.

As the knife drops out of my hand, I instantly flip over onto my stomach—adrenaline distracting me from the fact that the first seven-inch wound is gaping open—to try to use my decimated hands to struggle to my feet and get away from my attacker. I can only get to my hands and knees, though, before he pounces on my back.

He still hasn't spoken; he isn't about to let up, either.

The time it took for me to spin over and prop myself even slightly up was all he needed to grab the large knife blade that had slipped from my hand. In a swift, violent motion he snakes his left arm around my waist and pins me down with his weight to begin, once again, rapidly stabbing me over and over with his right hand.

I am trapped for good now, unable to defend myself in any way. All I can do is endure blow after vicious blow. I thought he was relentless before, but now he is swinging even more quickly and violently. It is as if he has crossed a point of no return, and now every frustration life ever handed him is being taken out on me in rapid-fire, nonstop stabs.

Trying to get my bearings after all the struggle, I lift my heavy head to see my dog Maggie right in front of me. I'd assumed this 70-pound black lab with a mean bark would help should I ever face an intruder. Now, as I endure stab after stab, my would-be attack dog is just inches away, doing nothing.

Why aren't you trying to help? I think.

The look she gives me might explain it. I have never seen a dog look so shocked in my life; Maggie's face registers utter confusion, helplessness, panic.

I relate.

The steel blade keeps slamming into the back of my head, then my back and shoulders. Ten stabs to my head. Seven to my right shoulder.

Then come the most devastating blows of all.

Perhaps me lifting my head when I looked at Maggie gave my attacker new inspiration. Suddenly, he aims for the base of my neck, the most accessible spot to try to sever my spinal cord. Urr. Urr. Urr. Urr. Over and over he slams the blade into that zone in rapid succession, sending electric-like shock waves with each of the vicious six or seven stabs. I've never before experienced pain like the sharp twinges I feel shooting throughout my body. Unaware how severe any of my wounds are, I am most concerned about these stabs—especially when the last one seems to hit the mark and I collapse face first onto the floor.

Lying flat on my stomach with my face on the ground, I find I can't move. I try. I can't.

I'm paralyzed. The knife damaged my spine, and now I'm paralyzed.

Game over.

Or so I think.

CHAPTER 5

"IT DOESN'T MATTER ANYMORE, I'M DEAD!"

Helpless, I lay motionless other than struggling to catch my breath.

For the first time, the stabbings cease. At last, my attacker speaks.

"Where are the keys and where is the money?" he grunts.

Are you kidding me? I think. *All this is for money —something I don't even keep in the house?*

Lying flat on my face gasping for air, I respond, "I don't have any money, and my keys are in the kitchen."

He leaves me on the floor and runs into the kitchen to look for the keys to my 2004 Ford Excursion he'd likely spotted sitting in my driveway. I try to search my mind for some kind of plan, but I don't have long before he comes back, unable to find the keys and fighting mad.

"Where are the keys and where is the money?" he spits at me again, stabbing me once in retaliation before grabbing my badly injured right hand to drag me toward the kitchen.

In excruciating pain, I'm mid-drag as I repeat, "I don't have any money, and my keys are in the kitchen."

He drops me flat on my face and goes back into the kitchen to look for the keys. *I gotta try to get up*, I think, but my body is dead weight, stuck to the ground. I can only move my head, and barely.

It's while he rummages in the kitchen this second time, getting more and more angry about not being able to find the keys, that I begin thinking about Caitlin and Noah. I visualize their school photos sitting proudly on our fireplace mantle, out of my line of sight but clear in my mind's eye.

That's when I make that plea about my kids, and he responds only by racing back to stab me more, perhaps getting in a punch or two but never addressing my plea. He seems focused only on his fury that he can't find the keys, which are unintentionally hidden under a piece of paper.

It is here, face down on my own floor enduring more blows despite having begged for my life based on my children, that I know ultimate hopelessness. Hopelessness, I discover, is no longer having the ability to see beyond my circumstances or do anything about them.

I'm finished.

My attacker, however is not.

He violently grabs my bleeding hand again, this time dragging me all the way into the kitchen. Then, he makes his broken-record demand a third time.

"Where are the keys and where is the money?" he insists.

Seriously?

A flash of anger surges through me. I am done begging.

You have just ruined my life, I think.

Fury and disgust overtake me. His actions, selfishness, heartlessness, violence—everything I know about him in this moment—have destroyed my hopes and dreams. No matter what he might get from the house when he's finished with me, he will take one thing with him for sure: my long-held vision for a happily-ever-after life.

So with the last of my strength, I lift my head toward my attacker. I want him to look me in the eye and sense my anger for everything he has just done. Gasping for one deep breath, with every ounce of disgust I can muster before my voice fades, I answer, "It doesn't matter anymore, I'm dead!"

Now, all that is left for me to do is lower my head onto the cold ceramic tile kitchen floor, pray my final prayers, and wait for there to be no more life.

CHAPTER 6
FINAL PRAYERS

I'll pretend I'm dead.

It's a fitting thought. I kind of feel dead. I've used the last of my energy, and my cheek is growing cold against the chilly tile.

My attacker buys it, apparently. He steps over me and out of the kitchen to head back out the entryway and upstairs to rummage for what he can find.

For the first time, I drift toward passing out. I'm losing a lot of blood; I can feel myself lying in it. I'm aware, though, that death is trying to push the life out of me and might succeed if I lose consciousness. That shocks me.

What are you doing? Stay awake, I think to myself.

Throughout this experience, I've only had time to react to it. Now, unable to take physical action other than staring at the bottom of the kitchen wall missing its paint trim along the floor line, I have my first chance to respond to it. So I go to prayer.

I want to ask God for something here in my lowest moment. It isn't for Him to send help. It isn't "deliver me." It isn't "catch the criminal." It's just for Him. I want to feel close to Him; I want to know He is close to me.

God, just let me know You are here, and You see me right here. Let me know that You were not surprised by this like I was, that this didn't catch You off guard. Give me a sign, please. Let me see angels. Let me hear Your voice. Let me see lights.

I pause, close my eyes, and wait for God's response to this horrible wrong that has been allowed.

Silence.

No signs. No sights of angels on assignment. No Bible verse with a promise to hold onto pops to mind; no bright lights or vision of heaven appear. In fact, I've never felt more alone. Even Maggie has disappeared. She probably followed the attacker upstairs.

How can it be that no one is helping when I need it most—not even my black lab?

Then hopelessness turns into a deep, dark kind of loneliness; I start to think about how I won't be found for some 17 or 18 hours, until church Tuesday night. Who will be the first to discover I've been murdered?

It's going to be Aaron, I think; he's our youth pastor who lives around the corner. When I don't show up for church, he will come looking for me and find my body in this pool of blood.

Perhaps I slip toward losing consciousness again, then back. I begin trying to visualize heaven and the reality that in a matter of minutes, if not seconds, my body will be lifeless on this floor, but my spirit will be alive elsewhere.

I want to be ready. I need to make sure I'm right with God.

Knowing I'm about to face a Holy God, I become aware of the stark difference between us. My mind races to every man's battle: lust and pornography. I've spent years fighting this battle. I think back 14 years to when, in reading Hebrews 12:16-17, the sense of being a man on the outside of God's will, looking in, by feeding those desires scared me. I resolved from that day forward to overcome them with His strength.

But that was 14 years ago; why is it coming up now? Why do I feel dirty again?

My mind flashes back to morning time, when Sarah was leaving and I felt rejected by her. Dealing with rejection has always been a struggle for me; today, though, that battle had turned darker than usual. I had contemplated turning to something other than my wife—the Internet—and just the thought alone made me feel so dirty.

I need to be washed. I need to be forgiven. He is Holy, and I am so unholy. So I pray.

God, I keep falling. I'm so sorry I thought about that stuff this morning. Make me clean. A…Amen.

Again, I start to pass out. Again, it's just for a moment, and then I come back with a new level of awareness. This is it, I realize. I don't have much life left in me. I'm down to my final act on this earth: praying for my family.

My beautiful wife will be a widow.

My young children will grow up fatherless.

It's so awful, realizing the full impact of what has happened here. I have to at least pray for the family I'm leaving behind.

My wife is the most important person in my life, and God intended this. I'm aware I'm supposed to love Sarah as Jesus Christ loves His Bride, the Church—and I've failed. I've allowed my ego and pride, my selfish desires, to stop me from loving her right.

God, please let Sarah know how much she has meant to me, I pray, my heart heavy with regret. Will you please let her know what I should have told her myself this morning—that I love her?

Next is Caitlin—she's only eight years old. How much will she even remember me? And who's going to be there for her the way I would be? I'm so aware of the unique father/daughter bond I hold with Caitlin. She is so much like me in so many ways, and all I want to do is hug her one last time and remind her of how beautiful she is, inside and out. I want to hold her in my arms and pray with her one last night that God will keep her in His will all the days of her life.

But I can't, and it breaks my heart that I'm not going to be there to watch over her while she grows into a woman. No little girl should ever be fatherless. How will she know how incredibly precious she is to her Heavenly Father if her earthy father is gone from her life?

God, become the Father to my daughter. Take care of every jerk who would ever try to put his hands on her the way I would take care of him. Keep her pure.

Noah. At age twelve, he's old enough to remember me for sure, and he has just entered that age where we are having the most meaningful conversations we've ever had. There is no greater feeling for a father than having your nearly teenage son climb into your recliner and nestle himself next to you, just because he wants to be close to his father.

I remember watching my son preach his first sermon at age ten. He preached about Abraham being told to sacrifice his beloved son Isaac. I remember telling Noah that if God ever asks you to let go of something you love so much, it is only because He has something greater He wants to give to you or He wants to lift your empty hands in worship to a faithful God. That story is the first time the word worship is mentioned in the Bible, and it's attached to letting go of someone who is dearly loved. Now, that idea is about to become all too real to Noah.

I'm worried about my boy. How will he respond to my murder? I've seen anger, bitterness, and hurt destroy the best of men, and now my twelve-year-old may have to battle these emotions. I only hope he will draw close to God in the aftermath.

Don't let him be angry at You, Lord. Don't let him blame you for what happened to me. Let him live, serve, and worship You all the days of his life. Please God . . .

I'm not really expecting to hear anything; I'd already given God a chance. But four very distinct words come anyway—loud, clear as day, and interrupting me mid-sentence as I'm trying to get out my last words of prayer for Noah before my final heartbeat stops me.

"THEY STILL NEED YOU."

CHAPTER 7
I'VE GOT TO LIVE

I'm still alone, bleeding profusely, and a split second out from finishing the final prayer I have to get through before I can relax and await heaven. But then, it's as if a light switch has been flipped on.

One minute I'm writing the end of my story. Four words later, I've got to live.

Someone needs me. My kids. My wife. Maybe others. *Don't give up,* I tell myself, and I feel the fight in me return; there's just no room for sad, defeated, dying me. *I've got to figure this out. I've got to get out of this mess. I can't quit.*

Turning my head to try to get my bearings, I see that the blood pooling beneath me is starting to spill down the steps.

The steps to the side door of my house.

There's my exit.

I'm no longer thinking about my attacker, who's ransacking the rooms upstairs. All sounds and details are drowned out by the urgency of the only things that matter: I'm needed, and now is the time to make a move. I must defeat the hopelessness that had convinced me I was dead.

I have to get up.

Moments ago, I could barely lift my head to try to face my attacker; he'd had to drag me to get my limp body in motion right before I hurled what I thought would be my last words at him. Now, somehow, I'm getting up. I'm moving as fast as I can, but everything seems like it is in slow motion. I'm beginning to slide on the ground to get to my knees when I become aware of an extremely weird feeling coming from my stomach area.

Something is not right.

As I'm looking around to see how I'm going to stand up, my left hand goes to feel my stomach area to try to figure out what the pulling and pinching feeling is.

Oh man.

Oh MAN.

I am feeling, then holding my intestines, hanging out from the gaping wound where my attacker slashed open my abdomen when I launched myself upon him from the stairs.

That first stab had disemboweled me.

Noooo—this cannot be happening! I'm going to have to carry my internal organs outside my body as I attempt to escape.

But there's no time to think I can't do that—I can. I must. *They still need me.* So I claw my way up, leaving bloody handprints on the walls as I use them to give me leverage to get to my feet in the slippery pool of blood now covering the first two steps down. Then, somehow, I'm walking. I have no idea how I'm doing it, but I don't care. I just want to get to the other side of the two doors in front of me.

Paying no attention to the fact my fingers are no longer attached to tendons and nerves, I unlock and inch open the interior door. Then I swing it open; I can now glimpse the world outside my home through the thick black bars of the exterior security door. Anticipating being grabbed from behind at any moment, I feel my heart racing faster than ever as I turn the dead bolt and unlock the door knob. I'm so close but still, surviving seems a million miles away.

Yet, somehow I make it out of the house. Throwing the door wide open, I begin making a mad dash, tripping over my feet, trying to stay upright as I stumble toward a neighbor's house, calling "Help me! Help me! Help me!" Dressed only in a pair of gym shorts, still holding my insides so they don't fall to the sidewalk, I'm desperate to survive.

I might live. I might make it.

"Help me! Help me! Help me!" I repeat as I climb the steps toward my neighbor's steel security door, identical to the one I'd escaped from at my own home just seconds before. Somehow, I make it to the white plastic chair outside his door and collapse onto it.

"Help me. Someone help me." My voice is weak; still, I see the curtains move, then my neighbor opens the inside door while standing safely behind the deadbolted security door. Surely this ends now; finally, my desperation to live will be rewarded. So clutching my intestines, I begin standing to my feet.

"Let me in," I say hoarsely. "Let me in. Help." I just need to get inside my neighbor's house, and then I will be safe. I've made it this far, and I'm now just two steps away from being helped.

But my neighbor doesn't seem to be unlocking his deadbolt.

"Come on, man. Let me in," I plead, beginning to panic as the seconds tick by. I'm aware my attacker most likely knows I've escaped; at any moment, I think, he will be coming to finish me off.

Still, just as quickly as hope reappeared when I opened my door, it disappears when my neighbor walks away without opening the security door.

Noooo.

I fall to the ground and curl up in a fetal position, completely helpless.

My only chance of living appears to have ended.

CHAPTER 8

LEADING WHILE SUFFERING

It's after 3 a.m. when I yell for help on my neighbor's porch in the inner city.

What if the shoe were on the other foot?

At that dark hour, would I have risked my own family to let in a guy covered in blood and hollering that he's been attacked—not knowing where the attacker is, only that he is capable of turning a healthy man into a bloody mess?

Would you?

I'm not capable of processing this in the moment, of course. All I know is when I'm finally in contact with a live, sane human being, I don't get the kind of help I want; instead, I am left outside on the porch just yards from where my manic attacker could come charging out at me any minute. All I can do curled up in the fetal position on the sandpapery indoor/outdoor carpet that lines my neighbor's porch is listen to him call 911 on the other side of the locked security door.

"Send the police. I need an ambulance."

"108 Montana Street[ii] in Highland Park. Hurry."

"Yes."

"No."

"No. Come on, lady. Just send help."

For heaven's sake, I'm *bleeding* here.

"What's the problem?" I call from the floor of the porch. "What's going on?" My neighbor also is growing frustrated and getting louder as the operator doesn't seem to understand him.

"He's on my porch."

"Yes."

"I don't know."

"I don't know."

"Hurry up."

"I don't know."

I am losing patience as fast as I'm losing blood.

"Just give me the phone, I'll talk to her." I call out. "You guys have got to hurry up. Just give me the phone. Give me the phone!"

[ii] Address changed to protect privacy.

My neighbor's muffled voice answers from the other side of the security door.

"Hold on, man, they are coming," he calls. "Hang in there."

I'm trying, but I'm beginning to get cold, even though it is nearly 90 degrees outside. The chill creeping over my body convinces me, again, that I'm not going to make it. This time, though, I am not alone. My neighbor may be unwilling to come out or let me in, but talking with him opens up a vital opportunity to relay information to my family.

"Tell my wife I love her!" I call, desperately. "My kids too!" Whew—at least my family will get these final messages.

"Help is on the way," he replies through the glass.

Then I start to think about the neighbor himself. I don't know this man very well, just enough to say hi in passing. Does he know God? I've never had the chance to ask him about his faith, and I want him to know the same things I want my kids to know.

"Tell my kids the greatest decision they can make is to live for Jesus Christ!" I call to him, hoping the message to my kids will have some sort of impact on him. I repeat my messages for my family and about God a few times, anticipating the light of heaven in between.

I see lights, all right, but they're swiveling red blue, red blue as a police car pulls up. Two officers approach, shining their flashlights at me.

They pause; their eyes go big at the sight of my blood-soaked figure huddling under the porch light and holding my intestines in my hands. I can tell the kind of shape I'm in just by the shock on their faces. I can almost hear them thinking—what did that? And if it did that to him, what could it do to me?

"Help me," I whisper.

Despite being stunned, one of them gets close to me on the porch floor and starts asking me questions.

"Do you know who did this?" he asks.

"No."

"Is he still there?"

"I don't know."

"What does he look like?"

"Bald head, stocky black man."

Keeping me talking is an effort, I realize, to keep me conscious as they try to figure out what to do next. The officers are deathly afraid of going through my house; they'd never seen anything like me, so covered in blood they can't even tell what race I am. Plus they'd arrived to scenes where people had a fraction of my injuries and didn't make it. So keeping me alive is their priority. But I'd find all this out later; in the moment, I have no such perspective. I just know I badly need encouragement—that I'm safe, that I'll survive, that justice will be served, something—and just like with my neighbor and even my dog, I'm getting only fear.

I don't need fear.

I'm good there.

An ambulance pulls up next, waking other neighbors who start to peek out of their own doors. The paramedics approach, noticing that my dog Maggie, who is covered in my blood herself, has shown up to stand guard over me. I don't even realize she's there, since I am focused on the hope that I'll see the kind of confident action I'm craving, now that the paramedics are on the scene.

Not so much.

As the two paramedics consider my bloodied figure, they pause to chat with each other about how slippery and heavy they think I will be. If I weren't dying, it might be funny; I'm lying there wearing only shorts, bleeding profusely with my insides on my outside, listening to this conversation about the paramedics' big challenge of this night: lifting up the stabbed guy.

Really? *Really?*

"He's too big to be carried off the porch," one says.

That does it. I'm done in a new way, now. Clearly, if I want to live, I'm going to have to lead.

"I didn't make it this far to have you kill me," I tell them hoarsely. "Listen . . . you two get up here and get one side of the stretcher."

My neighbor is next. "You, behind the door!" I call to him. "You need to *man up* and *get out here* to keep me balanced."

I guess being ordered around by the bloody guy helps.

The paramedics approach, and a small group of neighbors make their way out from behind the safety of their homes to help. As I drift out of consciousness, they work together to get me onto the stretcher and down off the porch.

"Can you hold your intestines?" the male paramedic asks, and I do before I drift out of consciousness as they move me down off the porch. Then the pain in my abdomen jolts me back to awareness as they push the stretcher into the ambulance; the pinching sensation is getting worse.

Once we're in the vehicle, the paramedics pick up their discussion without the kind of urgency I'm looking for in this moment.

"Which hospital should we take him to?" I hear one paramedic ask the other. "Henry Ford or . . . ?"

"I'm not sure," she replies. "Maybe. . ."

Are you kidding me?

"Listen, just get me to one of them," I interrupt. "Come on guys, get going! I've got to live. If you don't just go, it won't be the guy who killed me but you for taking too long. JUST GO!" Yelling this takes every last ounce of strength I have, and I lose consciousness again.

The next thing that jolts me awake is the noise of the ambulance doors opening and me being offloaded at the hospital. The medical team is ready, and right away, it's grab there, pull here, what's your name, do this *stat*, get that *stat*, we're going to take good care of you sir, as the large group of doctors and nurses quickly race me into the emergency room. The next few minutes are a blur as I'm given a dose of pain meds, X-rays are taken and I'm prepped for surgery before being moved into the operating room, clinging to life.

"Kevin, can you hear me?" I hear a woman in the distance, shouting so her voice can be heard above the emergency surgery preparations.

"Yeah," I respond.

"Do you know your wife's phone number? We need to contact her."

"Yes," I say, giving her the number with some relief. It's up to them now to let Sarah, who is nearly 600 miles away, know what is going on.

Okay.

At last.

Knowing I've done everything I possibly could have to get to this point, I'm at peace. It seems like I'm a million miles from my kitchen floor, where I lost all hope and stopped fighting to live. But to still be alive—to have escaped, to have gotten help at last, and now to be lying on this table with all these doctors around me— brings a sense of comfort to me. Life is no longer dependent on me winning the fight or getting out of my house; the future now belongs to Someone Else. So as the anesthesiologist places a mask over my nose and mouth, I take my last deep breath and send up one more prayer before succumbing to the medicine.

Okay, God. I've made it this far. It's up to You, now.

CHAPTER 9

SARAH'S FIGHTING WORD

Minutes after I gave the woman at the hospital Sarah's number and just hours after she'd arrived in Rockford, Illinois, my wife hung up the phone and dropped to her knees in her parents' kitchen.

"Jesus," she whispered desperately. "Jesus. Jesus."

She didn't know any details. The caller only told her she needed to get to the hospital right away so she can be given information about her husband. Information *about* her husband, not *from* her husband? What did *that* mean? She figured they must have spoken with me—how else could they have gotten her cell number, listed in my phone as "Mrs. Hottie"—so why couldn't she? But the hospital caller insisted she wasn't allowed to give any information over the phone, no matter how Sarah pressed.

"Am I going to drive seven hours and get there for you to tell me he is dead?" my wife had asked. Then the woman said if Sarah could send someone there, the hospital could release information to that person with her permission. So she arranged that, hung up, and sank to her knees.

"Jesus. Jesus. Jesus."

You can learn a lot about a person from her first response to crisis. Sarah didn't scream or run to her parents right away; she knew she needed to go to God first. It was a reflex, dropping to her knees and calling on the name of Jesus over and over. Then, my wife got up and shifted right back into the same focused packing mode she'd been in when she'd left me at our house less than twenty- four hours before.

From the beginning, Sarah says, God gave her just enough of what she needed, hour by hour, to get her through the next stretch. One way was through Pastor Tim insisting on being the go-between for information, coordinating with our youth pastor Aaron, the primary person to whom the hospital would release information. So she learned early on that I was attacked, but she didn't learn how bad it was. For example, when Aaron walked into the hospital and said, "I'm here for information about Kevin Ramsby," the woman looked him straight in the eye and told him, "Here's the thing: his wife needs to get here because he's not going to make it." But God worked through our pastor to protect Sarah from that detail while she was driving back so she could focus on hope—that I'd been talking, and that I'd been rushed into surgery.

Surely doctors wouldn't rush me into surgery if the situation were hopeless, she thought.

So she woke her parents with the news, explaining that she needed to go to me immediately. "We're going with you," her father said. So her mother began to dress and Sarah went to wake up our children.

"Dad's hurt," Sarah told Caitlin and Noah quietly as the kids rubbed their eyes. "We need to head home to see him." Minutes later, they got on the road and Sarah began calling friends and family for prayer, using as vague words as possible to try to protect Noah and Caitlin;

she'd asked her sister to call my mother so Mom could learn more details out of earshot of the kids.

Then just 10 minutes into my surgery back home, Sarah got a call that gave her the next dose of hope: she found out no vital organs had been critically hurt and that her husband *is expected to live*. Later, she will underline those last words in her journal.

"This was HUGE when you have a seven-hour trip ahead of you. Thank you Jesus!" she wrote.

When Sarah hung up from that call, her mom tapped her on the shoulder and gestured toward the back. My wife turned around to see Noah crying softly in the back seat, trying not to let her know he could hear her. Despite Sarah having worked to choose her words carefully, Noah had picked up on his dad being seriously hurt, and he was scared beyond what is reasonable for a child.

The wrong committed against me had begun its impact on my entire family.

So my wife began making her way back to our son, stepping over bags hastily thrown into her parents' van to hit the road as quickly as possible. Making it to Noah's side, she leaned over him and Noah could tell she was holding back tears herself as she told him what she'd just been told: that I was expected to live.

"Dad's going to be okay," she reassured him, hoping that would hold true. "He's going to be okay."

Sarah held our son the best she could in a moving vehicle, and they cried together for a minute, wordlessly united in recognizing that although we'd all thought we were untouchable, working safely in the inner city for years, it wasn't so. The bubble of security had burst.

Back in Detroit, doctors were working frantically. I don't remember this part, but I found out later from a kind nurse that when I got to the hospital, I'd looked at the medical team and said, "I am on a mission from God. I have to live. You have got to save me." Used to dealing with people who were strung out or hysterical, they thought there was something different about me, and one of the doctors made a dead-serious call to arms about it.

"Listen, I have no idea who this man is or what mission he is on," he told the rest of the team. "But this guy just fought for his life to get here, and we have got to do our part to make sure whatever that mission is, he can do it."

So they worked hard and well to overcome multiple hurdles, including the trouble they had intubating me due to the stab wounds that went through my mouth. Three or four hours into putting my abdomen back together, they thought they were finally there. So they couldn't figure out where the blood still pooling on the operating table was coming from—until they rolled me over, discovered the wounds on my back, shoulders, and neck, and realized I'd been stabbed 15 or 20 more times than they'd thought.

They'd never seen anyone with that many stab wounds.

So instead of finishing, the medical team geared up for hours of more surgery, without even being able to get to my hands; it's all the doctors could do to get me closed up before the blood loss won. But they did, and when my in-laws' van finally pulled up to the hospital late Tuesday morning, the survival surgeries were over.

Sarah's parents dropped her at the front door. My wife, of course, wanted to see me first; she didn't know what the kids might need to be protected from seeing. Her brother Caleb met her at the door to walk her to my room.

"He's out of surgery," he told her as they made their way up the elevator to my floor. "He actually looks pretty good, Sarah." Caleb, like Sarah herself, is not known for pulling his punches, so his assessment was encouraging.

Caleb, though, had been at the hospital for hours with the growing number of friends and family who'd gathered to pray, so he'd been exposed to the dire sense that I might not live. Sarah, on the other hand, entered the room having spent seven hours training her eyes on hope and any glimmer of God she could see. So while she was filled with love and thankfulness at what awaited her—there was her husband at last, and I was alive—she also was jolted at the sight.

It was bad.

She'd assumed she'd see someone looking like the man she loves. Instead, she couldn't see me for the bandages. Head—wrapped up. Another white bandage wound around my neck. The blankets were pulled up, and everything was white gauze. She didn't see hands at all—the wrapped-up appendages extending from my arms appeared to be fingerless.

For the first time, looking at the mummy in the bed, it hit Sarah how traumatic a thing her husband had been through. The instant she laid eyes on me, she realized she'll never be able to fully understand what the attack was like, that the physical—all she'd focused on until that point—was not what she needed to be worried about most. Who was in that bandaged head now?

"Is he even going to be the man I once knew?" she couldn't help but wonder, even when I opened my eyes for a moment.

Then, God gave her the next dose of hope.

I winked at her.

The wink—Sarah calls it "my little wink-blink thing"—was the kind I give her across a crowded room to connect with her, to let her know I know she's there, even if we're both busy with others. She's always known my smile is for everyone, but that wink is always and only for her.

"He knows I'm here," she thought with relief. "He recognizes me."

To be honest, like most of the next week, I don't remember it at all; Sarah would tell me about it later. I'm just recounting for you what God did for Sarah through me without me even being aware of it.

When our first response is prayer, God can do amazing things in our lives.

CHAPTER 10

GOD'S PROMISE

The rest of Tuesday was a blur for Sarah. Once she left my room, she walked past the familiar faces praying in the lobby to tell the kids it wasn't a good time to see me, and to send them with her parents to stay with family in the area for the time being. From there, she went on adrenaline as others steered her this way and that. Dr. Renny Abraham, a close family friend who had called Sarah with information from the surgical team on her ride back from Rockford, got her settled nearby into an apartment for families of certain patients, throwing it on his credit card. That would help Sarah keep the regular schedule Pastor Tim suggested for her from the get-go, so she could provide some semblance of normalcy for our family in the days ahead.

"Be with Kevin during the day," Pastor Tim advised, "and sleep at night."

That, it turned out, was easier to say than do. Having gone nonstop since the call from the hospital woke her up 600 miles away in the wee hours of the morning, Sarah was exhausted by the end of that first day, but she couldn't calm down. It was, after all, her first nighttime with the new awareness that anything horrible that could happen, just might. In fact, it had. So unsurprisingly, Sarah found herself too scared to sleep.

Again, you learn a lot about a person from her response to crisis.

When my wife found herself in total fear mode facing her first night after her husband had been stabbed nearly to death, she began praying in the Spirit and opened her Bible. She turned to Psalms, and right away God gave her a passage to stand on:

> He rescued me from my powerful enemy, from my foes, who were too strong for me. They confronted me in the day of my disaster, but the LORD was my support. He brought me out into a spacious place; he rescued me because he delighted in me. (Psalm 18:17-19)

To Sarah, that was a promise. The wife I so desperately wanted to let know I love her believed with all her heart that the Lord was telling her He delights in me, purposely saved me and planned to keep me around for a long time. In other words, she went *right* to faith for her encouragement, and after a bit, God's presence calmed her enough to let her crash for the night. Of course Sarah had no idea what was ahead, but from the point she heard God's promise on, she was completely willing to live the oft-quoted words of Holocaust survivor Corrie ten Boom:

"Never be afraid to trust an unknown future to a known God."

CHAPTER 11

THE TRIANGLE

It's a good thing Sarah had confidence in the Lord and what she'd heard from Him about me; she'd need that faith desperately during the first week of drastic ups and downs in the hospital, when the idea I'd be okay looked pretty iffy.

I was completely incoherent and on machines to keep me alive. Meanwhile, doctors were using phrases like "if he makes it," telling her though I'd survived surgery, this could happen, that could happen, plus "we don't really know what kind of person he'll be when we get him off the machines." Old friends warned her I'd probably experience a significant personality change—I'd be mean to her, most likely. The small, still voice of the Holy Spirit easily could have been drowned out by what people around her were saying.

Or by fear, exhaustion, and being overwhelmed. So many incredibly tough decisions were put on Sarah's slender shoulders that first week, starting with who to contact, what to tell the kids, and how much information to give to whom. All this in between answering questions from investigators who at first treated her as a possible suspect—the wife just *happens* to be out of town when the husband is stabbed, hmm—and taking endless phone calls from around the country as the news spread.

Sarah had a lot of help: our pastor's wife Cindy stayed by her side during the days at the hospital, other women from church stayed with her at night in the apartment while my mom stayed with me, and friends brought food, took the kids for playdates, and stayed close in case she needed anything. But there are only so many burdens others can take off you when you're dealing with the scariest days and decisions of your life.

Sarah was on pins and needles as she signed permission for blood transfusions. I'd lost so much blood—would I survive? Then doctors offered her two choices—putting my traumatized body back under for more surgery, or letting my yet-untreated hands atrophy, which would likely make at least two of my fingers useless. Fingers that had slipped a ring onto hers 14 years earlier; fingers that had held our children when they were born.

"He'd want you to try to save them," she told the doctors.

Then I started to run this crazy fever, and for an excruciatingly long time, doctors couldn't figure it out. My intestines were cut open—was I septic? So my wife prayed through that ordeal while the fever raged in response to an allergy the doctors didn't know I had until they got me off codeine. Next she faced my harrowing transition from a ventilator to breathing with just small nasal cannulas.

"Oh my gosh, you don't know how to breathe," Sarah thought, watching me struggle to get air in and out while a machine made a warning sound whenever I got a touch out of rhythm. *"Okay—let's do this together."*

"In . . . out . . . slowly . . . focus," she told me, while I was too doped up on pain meds and sedatives to be in my right mind, yet reactive enough to freak out when the tracking machine beeped.

"In . . . out . . ." she'd repeat gently as I hyperventilated over and over in a panicked reaction to the beeping. "In . . . out . . ." until Cindy was crying softly in the corner, overcome by the fear and tension in the room. Can you imagine trying to coach an out-of-it spouse who barely understands you to do something that should be simple, but isn't? While alarms go off around you? For an *hour?* How do you keep your composure? How do you stay focused on what someone else needs, not on how you feel?

My wife is amazing. She patiently endured one of the hardest, most intense experiences of her life until a new nurse came in after a shift change and adjusted the machine so it wouldn't beep so easily. Without that stressor, my breathing and my wife's pulse both settled down, and Sarah quickly credited God with a miracle, writing in her journal: *"Ventilator is out! Praise you Jesus!!! Fever is down! Praise you Jesus!!! My husband is alive! Praise you Jesus!!! We all have more pep to our step! Praise You Jesus!!!"*

In fact, Sarah's journal is jam-packed with such love and praise for God; instead of getting bogged down in the unknowns, Sarah looked for God's fingerprints. For example, she listed 35 miracles she and Cindy identified in the situation, including a bathroom break on the agonizingly long ride from Rockford that may have kept her from being in an accident involving a truck rollover, which happened right where her parents' vehicle would have been if they hadn't been delayed.

She also made a list of how she felt I'd succeeded in letting her know I love her: the way I looked at her, or by finding out through the police what I'd been telling the neighbor. Even when I was frighteningly bug-eyed and thrashing about early on, resisting the machines that were helping keep me alive—during times when she'd journal plaintively that she wished God would throw in a lesson on reading my mind, along with lessons on patience in the storm—Sarah would look for the upside.

"I have to say in moments of tension, Kevin's agitation actually does my heart good," she wrote. *"He is a fighter and wants to get better."*

Sarah also drew the classic triangle in her journal with the word "husband" by the bottom left corner, the word "wife" by the bottom right corner, and the word "God" at the top. See, as much as Sarah loves me, she knows God must be the higher priority. She also knows that marriage works best in the tension of a perfect triangle, where the closer a husband and wife are to God individually, the closer they are to each other as well.

Sarah may not have had full access to me that first week in the hospital, but she knew how best to maintain our marriage anyway: by keeping close and tight to the top of the triangle.

CHAPTER 12

LAUGHTER FILLS
THE ROOM

Sarah's journaling of the days when I was out of it wasn't just gratitude, praise, and Bible verses. She also mentioned the big moment of each day (she recorded my first words as "I want to go home") and more entertainingly, several funny little details that made having so much to handle go down a little easier.

For Sarah, those moments became the medicine for her soul, the answer to the prayers to help her get through this. See, even when you're trusting God for a miracle, it's tempting to get stuck in the moment, to sink into pits of depression about the unknowns you face right then. But my wife knows you also can look for the lighter side, and healing can begin in laughter.

And sometimes, the funniest things are tucked into the most tragic.

For example, it started out horrific that I was stabbed. But it became kind of funny when I started to be able to speak and my answer for absolutely any question was, "Yeah, because I was stabbed a lot."

"How's your pain level?" a nurse asked.

"Eight—because I've been stabbed multiple times," I'd explain.

I'd complain of my hands hurting: "I was stabbed so much."

A few minutes later: "I was stabbed in the hands."

It got to the point where Sarah and Cindy giggled when I mentioned it. Same deal when I kept complaining about the water they gave me from sponges.

"Water, water," I muttered unappreciatively. "Now I want a Sprite."

Could I wait a few minutes for a different dose of pain meds?

"I really think a can of Sprite would . . ." and the girls would giggle.

Like the Bible says, a cheerful heart is good medicine. And the truth is, every funny moment was also a hopeful moment. Yes, I was repeating myself like Rain Man. Yes, I kept trying to make a case for pop being a better treatment for stabbing than pain meds.

But these loopy moments also revealed the progression of normalcy. Sure, I still had a tube down my nose, and was catheterized for waste elimination. But I could answer a question. I could follow up with conversation.

And soon, I started asking questions of my own.

"Where am I?" I asked at one point. Sarah told me Henry Ford Hospital.

"Oh. I thought I was in Oklahoma City."

My wife started to see I still had a grasp on my life; I still knew I was supposed to be in Oklahoma for the conference about church planting that week. Plus my personality was starting to show up.

"Itch my hip," I told my mom at one point, and she made a girly attempt. "No, itch it like a man."

Yes, people were amused, but they were grateful too. God had been faithful to what Sarah had heard from Him; I was still there, in more ways than one.

Then, in addition to slurring that I'd been stabbed multiple times and needed more refreshing beverages, I began asking for my kids repeatedly, more and more urgently.

"Where are the kids?"

"Are the kids okay?"

"I want to see the kids!"

It was Saturday—five days after the attack, and weeks since I'd last seen the kids before they'd gone to their grandparents' home for their summer visit. I was getting very antsy and a little wild, not wanting to wait anymore.

Between that, and me starting to complain that I wanted something to eat, it became clear I was on the upswing. Sarah had been waiting for me to come back to being more like myself before she brought the kids in, and now, I was showing signs I was ready.

It was time for the tubes that stood between me and seeing my kids to come out.

INTERLUDE

GOD SHOUTS IN OUR PAIN

Revealing the wrongs and what happened to me is vital to making room for God to use it for His greater purposes, and frankly, there would have been no real benefit to keeping it a secret even if I could have. Actually, I believe the Enemy uses secrecy to try to trip us up, since he certainly wants to hinder God from bringing good out of wrongs. So I've kept no secrets about what happened.

I wish I could say the same about acknowledging the hurts that came out of it. There, I let pride, old ideas about what it means to be a man, and misplaced shame delay me from stepping up for this crucial part of the process God has led me through.

No more.

To be honest, the hurts were fairly shocking to me. Much like I had no idea what was coming when I went to sleep to the hum of the air conditioning on the evening of August 3, 2009, I had no idea what was coming when I was excitedly looking forward to seeing my children for the first time after the attack.

Fixated only on connecting with my family—and having been basically out of it since I went under anesthesia for surgery—I was unaware of what they had been through in the days since the attack. I had no clue about Noah's scared ride in the back of the van, of my answered prayers that God let Sarah know I love her, none of it. Every ounce of my emotional energy was directed toward reconnecting with them; emotional pain wasn't yet on my radar.

I'd also felt very little physical pain since being awakened by the smashing glass the night of the attack—only the painful electric- like twinges while being stabbed in the back of the neck, then the sharp, pinching sensation from my intestines while on my neighbor's porch and in the ambulance. Otherwise, my adrenaline during the fight itself, then the medication in the days after, had made pain seem virtually nonexistent.

All that was about to change.

The common elements of life—physical, emotional, and mental well-being, family, ability to connect with others, work, finances, sense of security, parenting—ranged from ordinary to wonderful for me up until the attack. But what happened early in the morning August 4, 2009, devastated all of them. Each became like a battle zone after the attack, as the floodgates of pain opened wide in my life.

Hurt can't be ignored. C. S. Lewis had it right when he said, "Pain insists upon being attended to. God whispers to us in our pleasures, speaks in our consciences, but shouts in our pains."[iii]

Let the shouting begin.

[iii] C. S. Lewis, *The Problem of Pain*, rev. ed. (New York: HarperOne, 2015)

PART TWO

ACKNOWLEDGING THE HURTS

THE WOUNDS

CHAPTER 13

HURT INVADES

"Can you hear me, Kevin?" a voice asks. I remember hearing the nurse, though I was still too foggy to retain any visual memory.

"We want you to see your kids, but we have to remove the tube out of your nose and we are going to take out your catheter. Okay, Kevin?"

I nod. She calls a second nurse to assist.

"Kevin, we are going to take both tubes out at the same time. You are only going to feel the tube coming out from your nose. When I begin, I want you to exhale through your nose as it comes out. It's going to hurt, but it will only take a second. You ready?"

I nod back.

"Ok. Everyone, let's do this together. Kevin, breathe out through your nose ... NOW," she instructed me, as she and her partner began pulling.

Helloooooooo, Pain.

"OOOOWWWW," I let out an uncontrollable moan as I exhale, my eyes instantly flooding in reactive tears to the intense burning sensation in my nose. It kind of feels like I was just punched in the face, only this amped-up version of pain is like nothing I've ever felt before.

Then, as quickly as the agony comes, it begins subsiding. I'm functioning on my own again, free of tubes. And because of the sharp pain I've just experienced, I'm now alert.

Pain has a way of getting our attention like that.

A moment later, the agony is no longer even a thought; it's replaced by love and joy bursting to the surface when the nurses let Sarah know it's now okay for Noah and Caitlin to come and see me for the first time.

I can't wait to be close to my two precious children. I've been replaying visualizing their school pictures while pleading with my wrongdoer to let me live for their sake. Now, in just seconds, I'm going to finally get to see them in person. So when the door swings open, my eyes quickly find Noah and Caitlin across the filled, busy room.

But something is wrong.

I'm anticipating shared excitement and unabated joy.

I see fear.

In that split second, I realize this reunion will be different than I expected, and I'm instantly crushed. I'm not sure what they have been told, but I can read its impact in the obvious uncertainty, fear, and hurt in their eyes.

It's understandable, of course; after all, the last time they saw me we were laughing, playing games, and packing their bags for their trip to Illinois. Now that I'm scarred and bandaged, I'm sure I look like a scary mummy to them.

Still, considering my anticipation, the lack of mutual euphoria leaves a chilly void.

"Get over here, guys," I tell them. "Come closer; I need to see you." As they continue to hang back, I try to cut through the coldness with promises of future fun.

"Noah, I owe you a big fishing trip," I tell my son. "We are gonna go fishing. I owe you, bud!"

Next I turn to Caitlin, who is as hesitant as her brother.

"Come here, Princess," I urge her. "I love you so much. We're going to go on a breakfast date!"

Slowly, together, Noah and Caitlin began to nudge their way toward the head of the bed; when they finally get to me, love and joy takes over on my end, undeterred by the kids' hesitance.

"You guys are the greatest kids in the world," I tell them, on cloud nine as love overshadows the pain from the tubes and seeing the hurt in their eyes. "The both of you, give me a kiss." That's right—I make both pre-teens give me a kiss right on the lips, just inches away from stitches and wounds in plain sight. That's not exactly like me. Sarah, I find out later, is beginning to wonder if she let them see me too soon.

Today, my kids joke about how goofy I was that day. But in the moment, my affection and kissing, along with sights and smells in the hospital room, are almost as traumatizing to the kids as the attack was to me. So I try harder to lighten things up.

"Caitlin, I'm thirsty. Get the sponge and put it up to my lips. Come on, Noah, you too. Get a sponge with some water and give me a drink," I say, trying to make a game of giving drinks to their nearly murdered father in his hospital bed. "Isn't that cool?"

Cool wasn't really the word for it, looking back.

I would have been happy to have kept them there longer, but that first visit ended in minutes, with the kids being ushered away quickly so I could settle back down and so they wouldn't be overwhelmed.

As they start to leave, I catch more glimpses of their hurt in the quick disappearance of Caitlin's smile as she steps toward Sarah, and the slight quiver in Noah's lips as he too inches closer to his mom.

My boy is trying to be strong, I think to myself. *For ME.*

Noah and Caitlin disappear to the other side of that door different from the kids I remembered from three weeks before. They are afraid. They are sad.

They are deeply hurt.

They have become victims of the wrongs and hurt created by my attacker, even though they were hundreds of miles away.

CHAPTER 14

A PAINFUL CONFESSION

Seeing the kids again was awesome, despite the heartbreak. But as soon as the emotional high of that subsides, I discover another of the many wounds and hurts that can't be stitched up by doctors.

It's a shame thing. This may sound odd to some, but I know there are others who know what I mean—from men who have known what it feels like to lose a fight, to people who have been raped and wonder if it's their fault, even as people around them tell them it isn't. It's easy for me to see those people's innocence, but I also relate to the deeply personal sense of shame that can surround certain hurts.

For Sarah, though, mine comes as a total surprise.

The night after I see the kids, I am moved out of the ICU to what I am told is a room on a secure floor. This helps me calm down from what Sarah describes as a "bug-eyed paranoia" my attacker will return to finish me off. The next morning, Sarah has just found her way to this new room when I lose it.

My wife has been waiting for some sort of crash on my part—the question of when I'd break down about what happened rose multiple times in conversations with others while I was still loopy—and she didn't have to wait long. It's been fewer than twenty-four hours since I came out of the stupor of tubes and pain meds; it's also the first time it's been just the two of us since I became more myself.

And I'm weeping uncontrollably.

"What's the matter, Kevin? Are you okay?" Sarah asks. "Are you in pain? What do you need? Talk to me. What's wrong?"

My throat feels as if a baseball is lodged in it. At first, I can only cry hard, wave after wave of regret preventing my ability to speak while my mind fixates in on one specific, torturous moment the night of the attack.

I'm mentally looking at myself lying on the kitchen floor, having lost the physical fight, covered in blood, and 100 percent convinced my life is over. I couldn't move. I believed I was paralyzed. No one was around nor able to help me. My life and circumstances had gotten so bad that I concluded, "It doesn't matter anymore, I'm *dead!*"

My whole life, I'd understood that manhood means you not only throw punches, but you take them for yourself and those you love. You don't become blinded by circumstances, pain, and hurt, or convinced your wounds are beyond rescuing or recovery. When you're attacked, you fight. And you don't stop.

Yet during the attack, I had stopped. The words wouldn't stop ringing in my head throughout the long hours of that first night I was alert.

It doesn't matter anymore—I'm dead.
It doesn't matter anymore—I'm dead.
It doesn't matter anymore—I'm dead.
It doesn't matter anymore—I'm dead.
It doesn't matter anymore—I'm dead.

It's a wound that hurt more and more as the hours wore on through the night to where now, I want to talk. I want to share with my wife that I'm feeling I let her down, and I let Noah and Caitlin down.

It doesn't matter anymore, I begin hearing again in my head when finally, I fight through the shame to speak out loud.

"It does matter . . . It did matter . . . I'm SORRY, Sarah! I'm sorry, Sarah! I'm so sorry . . ." I say, sobbing more intensely as I repeat my regret over and over.

Now Sarah is scared. Remember, she'd been told I could wake up a totally different guy, and now she has no idea what I am talking about. Could there be some drastic secret I've kept?

"Babe, what are you sorry for? Please, talk to me," Sarah pleads, her eyes beginning to swell with tears.

"I'm sorry, Sarah. I'm sorry. I'm sorry that . . . that . . . " It takes everything in me to add the last two words to clarify what is hurting me so deeply. It's so hard to admit I am guilty of breaking a pledge made to God, my wife, and my family fourteen years earlier after watching my parents' twenty-five-year marriage end in a bitter divorce, when they gave up on each other. I want to tell Sarah that, but it feels like I can't, at first. I wasn't taught how to do it.

Then somehow, I can.

"I'm sorry that . . . *I quit.*" There, I said it. "I quit, and I am so sorry," I choke out through another downpour of tears and hurt.

My wife leans over to wrap her arms tight around me best she can. I am thankful for her love, but I need something else. Taking a deep breath, gaining my composure, I put the hard question out there.

"Will you forgive me?" I ask my wife.

Sarah doesn't hesitate.

"Of course I forgive you, Kevin," she replies. "But I still have no idea what you are talking about. How did you quit? When did you quit? What did you quit?"

I look her in the eye, trying to make sure every ounce of hurt, shame, and guilt in me is brought to light.

"I am sorry that I quit fighting *for* you," I say through the waves of hurt. "I'm sorry I quit fighting *for* us, *for* our kids, our future, our tomorrow."

"Things were so bad during the fight, I gave up and quit. I thought it was over. I couldn't get him off me, I couldn't move. I stopped fighting for everyone that I loved and what God still has in front of us. If I hadn't heard the words 'they still need you,' I wouldn't have even attempted to get up."

Okay. At last, it was out there.

Sarah, though, is mostly perplexed. She's relieved I am talking at last, and that I finally seem to be breaking free from confusion, euphoria, and paranoia to do something remotely normal. But she had been expecting my breakdown to be about why this happened to me; she wasn't expecting my first emotion to be guilt.

"Are you kidding me, Kevin?" she says gently but incredulously. "What in the world do you have to be sorry for? You didn't lose the fight, and you most certainly didn't stop fighting. You won. You are here today because you *kept* fighting. You don't owe me any apology, you didn't quit."

I need that from her so badly, and it is good to come clean and connect heart-to-heart with my wife again. The crying and conversation with Sarah help me move forward, though it will take years for this wound, disappointment, and hurt to finally heal in my life. Plus, there are many more hurts yet to be faced.

And unfortunately, that emotional moment with Sarah will be the last healing conversation I'll have for a while.

CHAPTER 15

WOUNDS FESTER IN DARKNESS

"Don't ask him questions."

"Don't bring up anything about the attack."

"It's not good for him to talk about it and keep reliving that night."

"He needs to heal. When he is made to revisit that night and what happened, it only reopens mental and emotional wounds that are trying to heal."

"Just listen. Don't try to get him to talk."

From the beginning, many people who spent time with me were cautioned against talking much about the attack. I didn't know about the warnings, but I could tell something was off when one of the faithful men from our church would stay by my side to give Sarah the ability to keep the ordinary day-night cycle our pastor recommended. The reason I was there, and they were there, was that I'd been attacked, and anyone who spent time with me quickly saw I needed help doing everything due to the damage—but we weren't talking about it.

The awkward silence just seemed so weird in the face of the magnitude of what had happened.

Physical Wounds

I was stabbed a total of thirty-seven times to the chest, throat, face, arms, hands, back, and shoulders, in one of the most violent crimes our city has ever seen. My body is covered in nearly four feet of scars; my stomach muscles are completely butchered and had to be patched together awkwardly. To this day, I'm reminded of the attack every time I struggle to use muscles forever damaged to get up out of a chair or sit up from bed.

And that's nothing compared to my hands. For nearly five months, I'd spend hours per day getting my vastly damaged fingers, which were locked in place by scar tissue, to bend and move—and all these years later, they still ache incredibly and constantly. Many times I've thought it would be so much better if I just got rid of my fingers, on my own, so that the discomfort would be over. I know I can't, of course; it is a hurt I'll have for the rest of my life.

But don't "make me" revisit that night? How could I *not* revisit that night?

To be fair, though, the fault for me not talking about my hurts was on me too; having believed my whole life I was to own my pain and hurts at any cost, I pulled back and built walls. The problem, though, was that being alone with my thoughts was mentally and emotionally dangerous; behind those walls, I began tearing myself apart for all the things I should have done in my life.

Mental and Emotional Wounds

It started with wanting to go back and redo that night. To redo that day. Then, I wanted to go back months and years and capitalize on opportunities to invest more into my kids and my family. And as I went further and further back without talking to others about my thoughts, I started drowning in regrets about the past.

Take my mom. It meant a lot that she flew in as quickly as she could to spend nights with me and give Sarah a break that first week. I didn't deserve her being there for me because I hadn't been there for her for more than a decade. Sure, we casually talked here and there, but not much; after she left my dad fifteen years before, I divorced myself from her.

I wanted to make it right. I wanted to tell my mom "I'm sorry." I wanted to hug her. I needed to talk. But I couldn't, and my emotional wounds seemed to be spreading and getting infected as I marinated, alone in my head, in that and other regrets of my past.

Dad, for example.

My father, who had died unexpectedly seven years before the attack, was my best friend, and in my formative years, my biggest role model. A "man's man" with enormous forearms that mimicked Popeye's from his decades of using hand tools as an electrician and builder, he was tough as nails. I don't remember ever seeing my dad cry while growing up; instead, he showed me not only how to be tough on the outside, but how to be tough on the inside as well.

Or so I thought. Years later, I'd find out that rather than letting hurts bounce off of him, he had actually absorbed the full effect of them like a sponge, particularly during his rough childhood and teen years. He never learned how to release hurts through conversation and honesty, turning instead to unhealthy choices to try to numb things out.

In the last year of his life, I had made the tough choice to intervene after he had become addicted to pain killers—his attempt to move forward while carrying hidden hurts. The intervention didn't go well; my dad was angry, hurt, and embarrassed that I surprised him with it. So the relationship I had with my father, my best friend, was severely damaged. He pointedly wrote me off (his will stated something to the effect of "My son Kevin is to get nothing") and worse, our relationship was never restored to the way it was before. At the time of the attack, I'd lived seven years regretting that I never went back to my dad to try to renew our father-son friendship. I was too scared. I had hoped time would heal the wounds. It didn't.

"And now it's too late," I thought darkly.

These are the sort of self-loathing thoughts I obsessed about, alone in my head, and I had years of such ruminations ahead. After the attack, it was a very long time—until about January 2015—before I could sleep much if at all, which further diminished my ability to cope or correct perspectives that drove me to darker and darker places.

The emotional and mental damage spilled over into my relationships too. Just like my skin, muscles, and hands are forever set differently, so am I. This quickly showed itself in the interactions I did—and didn't—have in the hospital.

Relational Wounds

Warned to shy away from talking about the elephant in the room, people around me mostly armed themselves with bright, meaningless things to say or humorous reminiscing. Sarah was glad to grab any light moment, but for me, with a decimated abdomen and a similarly shredded spirit, laughter was just painful, physically and emotionally. I began to turn away visitors who tended to make me laugh. It was so unlike the old me—the life of the party, fun-loving, and willing to do whatever to get a laugh. But the attack gave me a weight that caused me to become much more serious, which made it so much harder to connect with people.

Such struggles didn't end when I left the hospital, either. In the months and years that followed, I discovered that the attack generally hurt my ability to have and maintain healthy and needed relationships. Hinged on the words, "they still need you," life became a mission for me, and I lost interest in just hanging out and having conversations that weren't about helping people. I found I couldn't help seeing selfishness in most normal, day-to-day concerns. Frustrated and not wanting to judge, I pulled back more and more.

Ministry Wounds

The struggle to relate to people about ordinary life would affect my pastoral work too, obviously. Things were okay from the pulpit; in fact, sermons became my relational outlet. I felt free to talk about what happened there, as people can identify and relate to a hurt man with a message. One-on-one, though, was a different story. I struggled to connect with anyone who wasn't hurting, which is pretty limiting when you have a church full of people in all different places in life. Some began to question my ability to lead, and I began to think they were right, wondering whether I was too serious, too withdrawn now to be the kind of leader others would want to follow.

That hurt like crazy.

The impact on my work life went further than my limited ability to connect with people. For nearly nine months, I was not able to return to work in a full-time capacity. I tried for a while to balance both getting better and earning money, but it just wasn't possible.

"I can't do this any longer," I found myself saying under my breath. "Either I choose to focus on healing, or I have to figure out how to pay all these bills." With as much damage as I'd taken in the attack, I simply couldn't do both. "They still need me" seemed to show me where the priority was: no matter how much money I made, I'd be of little use if I stayed as physically, mentally, and emotionally wrecked as I was right after the attack. Clearly, I had to choose to get better.

But that came with a big price tag.

Financial Wounds

The inability to cover our bills and the unending financial stress we incurred after the attack drove us to the point where we eventually lost everything, including our beloved home at 110 Montana Street into which we had invested more than thirty thousand dollars. There went all of our savings.

A year after the attack, Sarah and I made one of the toughest decisions of our lives—to file for Chapter 7 bankruptcy—which we knew would create five to seven years of more hurt in our lives. With the bankruptcy came the ultimate sense of hitting rock bottom. In the financial world I was labeled a risk, irresponsible, not a good steward, a failure.

It hurt.

"I'm just a bankrupted, pitiful pastor," I began telling myself, and the idea grew whenever we faced the repercussions of our financial hurt, such as rejection after rejection trying to find a new home to rent since we could no longer buy.

Still, that wasn't the worst of it.

Security Wounds

My family went from living what felt like a sheltered life in a safe and stable home to having every sense of security stripped away from us. In addition to losing our house, we lost the sense of home itself; struggling with place after place, it would be years before we would feel safe again.

Plus, my wife and kids lost the husband and father they had always known.

In addition to serving as my nurse for months and months—including packing my wounds twice a day, a painful process of carefully changing gauze stuck to wounds left open to heal from the inside out—Sarah watched me become an emotional roller coaster. To this day she has to deal with a jumpy husband who now can be startled awake by anything—say, a slight creak in the floor—freak out, and have a really hard time calming down. In addition to being afraid of waking me up, Sarah now lives with a heightened sense of uncertainty, fear of unknowns, and fear of being a widow unlike anything she knew before that fateful night.

As for Noah and Caitlin, being overwhelmed with kisses and affections by a scarred and smelly figure in a hospital bed was just the beginning of having a dad who couldn't deal with emotions, change, and challenges like he used to. In time, I would see my hurts manifesting themselves in fear and paranoia, and invading the way I parented my kids.

The good news is, this would lead to one of the first times I'd break the silence that started in the hospital.

CHAPTER 16

COMING CLEAN WITH HURTS

I became paranoid that something would happen to my kids as a result of the attack, and they would grow up angry and rebellious because I had chosen to remain in the inner city. So before I even left the hospital, I decided to transfer my kids from their public charter school to the more protected environment of a private Christian school.

But that was the least of the changes Noah and Caitlin had to face. Being convinced I'd never see my kids again created a monster in me that needed every second of every day to be a meaningful interaction between me and them.

All of this came to a head one day when Noah, then fourteen and in ninth grade, and I had a disagreement. He had never done this before nor has he ever since, but in the middle of being addressed, he walked away and went to his room.

I lost it. I began weeping and wailing uncontrollably upon hearing his door shut.

"I can't do this, I can't do this," I cried out hysterically.

Noah instantly raced back down the stairs to where I was sitting in my recliner crying uncontrollably, and climbed into my lap.

"What, Dad? What, Dad?" he asked. "What can't you do? What's wrong? I'm sorry, I'm sorry!"

Even as he apologized, I knew it wasn't about what had just happened—and in that moment, I was finally able to put into words what had been fueling my intensity toward him and Caitlin.

"I almost lost you once, I can't lose you again. I am afraid I'm going to lose you again," I blurted out. "Not that something is going to happen to you or me, but to us. I love you son! I can't lose you to anger.

"I'm trying, Noah, I'm trying, Noah—I'm just so scared," I finally confessed.

Our whole family cried that night; it was the first breakthrough we'd shared as a family, and my most emotional moment since I'd asked Sarah's forgiveness for giving up on the family that first alert day in the hospital. Together, we recognized that hurt has this natural ability to fill every area of your life if not acknowledged. The good news, though, is as I shared this hurt and we embraced each other, I could sense a new healing begin in our lives.

More healing came when the painful, open wound of the financial devastation from the attack stopped bleeding. Was it when the discharge papers came, or debtors stopped calling? No. It was when I finally spoke publicly about our financial hurt leading to bankruptcy in a sermon three full years after the attack. That Sunday morning I cried, I acknowledged, and for the first time, that hurt began to heal.

As you can see, it took me a while to learn I needed to acknowledge my hurts; at first, I did the opposite. However, I came to discover that stuffing it down only increased the damage, as the wounds festered in darkness. C. S. Lewis, once again, put it best: "I have learned now that while those who speak about one's miseries usually hurt, those who keep silent hurt even more."[iv]

The truth is, the attack hurt like crazy, in every way. To this day, there is healing still needed and still happening. In time, though, I'd learn that acknowledging my hurts, like revealing the wrongs, is crucial to making room for God to change me on the inside while using wrongs and hurts to bring about His plans.

That isn't all it takes, though. Next up in making room for God to turn evil into good would be fighting a trust thing through with Him directly. See, I haven't yet mentioned the most painful hurt of all: the spiritual one.

It hurt so much that God allowed this wrong and so much pain in my life, and then it appeared that He wasn't even there for me through it.

This one cut deep; eventually I'd get to where I couldn't even pray or believe God for anything personally. It was a terrible, guilty secret; I felt like a cross between a Christian and a philanthropic atheist, committed to helping others in the name of Jesus but absent of a growing relationship with him. And here I'm a pastor.

Eventually acknowledging that hurt to some folks would, like with my parenting hurts and my financial hurts, be pivotal to beginning

---

[iv] C. S. Lewis, *The Collected Letters of C. S. Lewis, Volume III: Narnia, Cambridge and Joy 1950-1963*, ed. Walter Hooper (New York: HarperCollins, 2009)

to heal from it. But first, before I even left the hospital, a trial was in order.

It wasn't going to be my attacker I needed to accuse, challenge, and debate, however. It was the One who hurt me even more.

THE BIGGEST WOUND OF ALL

First installed in the mid-1940s, the old glass window pane stayed intact for years through hail, sleet, violent rain, snow, and heat. Even the pesky Detroit pigeons that would occasionally fly into the old glass were no match for it.

But despite surviving those threats, the window at 110 Montana Street was broken beyond repair and left scattered in pieces all over the floor on August 4, 2009. And it was far from the only thing shattered that night.

My faith had weathered some previous challenges too. I got rejected on both sides of this huge change in my life. After I started believing in God and surrendered my life to Christ, news traveled fast at my high school; I soon found the contents of the locker I shared with a buddy dumped in the middle of the hallway, a not- too-subtle sign from my friends they wanted nothing to do with someone they viewed as "religious." Then years later, when I asked for an extension on a paper in Bible college, professors tell me my priorities were wrong, I wouldn't make it more than a year in ministry, and I was wasting my time trying to become a pastor.

But God was there for me through those and many other storms, and my faith, like that old window for so many years, stayed firmly intact. I chose to follow God and His heart for people like me who have been overlooked and not given a chance. Really, it made sense; after all, He'd always been faithful, keeping His Word and never doing anything to make me question His character, ability, or love.

He didn't, that is, until the attack.

That night, in my darkest hour, I'd called upon God's great name and cried out for His promised help. He was all I wanted, all I needed. My thoughts went nowhere but to Him.

"God, just let me know You are here, and You see me right now," I'd prayed as I lay on my floor, helpless, bleeding. *"Let me know that You were not surprised by this like I was, that this didn't catch You off guard. Give me a sign, please. Let me see angels. Let me hear Your voice. Let me see lights."*

With all the faith I could muster up in that dying moment, I closed my eyes and waited. Full of anticipation, I completely expected and trusted God to not only hear, but to answer me. How did He make me aware of His presence? How did He let me know He was there, that He saw me in my moment of desperation?

He didn't answer me.

Now, recovering from the attack, I absolutely must confront Him about it; I can't possibly go on loving, worshiping, serving, and living for a God who deserts His own and doesn't keep His Word. To move forward in relationship with Him, I have no choice but to be very honest with God about what I see as the ultimate betrayal. In other words, I need to charge Him with abandonment— withdrawing support or help despite allegiance or responsibility.

Will He remain silent again? Will He answer for Himself? Will He prove me wrong in my charge?

Court is now in session.

PART THREE

TRUSTING GOD

GOD ON TRIAL

CHAPTER 17

INDICTING GOD

Let's start with what my charge is NOT, I clarify to God in my mind as I retreat further and further away from what is going on around me. I'm not charging You with being unfair, and I get that You didn't cause this. I understand that just because I'm a Christian doesn't mean I'm guaranteed life will be a walk in the park; I get that we're in a spiritual battle against a real Enemy, the one who has been out to get You and Your children ever since he was cast out from heaven.

So instead, my charge of abandonment is centered upon Your neglect to keep Your Word. You promised in Psalm 46:1 to be an ever present help in time of need. In Deuteronomy 31:6, Your Word says You will never leave us nor forsake us. But when I turned to You, when I prayed to You in my lowest moment—when I desperately needed You to do what You said You would do and be who You said You would be—I got silence.

What happened? Did I not follow some particular prayer formula? Was I supposed to begin with thanksgiving? Was I supposed to worship You like Job with words like "the Lord giveth and the Lord taketh, blessed be the name of the Lord?" to get your attention? Sorry if I missed that fine point. The thing is, I was hurt. I was dying. I was alone. So I prayed the best I could.

Do You even remember? Or did You forget me, too busy with all the other crises in the world to respond to the prayer of a dying man to a supposedly loving, all-knowing, and all-powerful God? I am honestly not trying to be rude or disrespectful. But I am so deeply hurt, and it isn't always pretty when we share our hurts.

For nineteen years I've lived for and loved You, I told the Lord. I've followed You. I've served You in places where many would never even think of visiting out of fear. More importantly, good times and bad, I always felt, sensed, and knew You were with me. This time, though, it was different. You left me all alone. To struggle. To quit. To stop fighting. To become hopeless. As far as I can see, You were nowhere to be found in my ultimate moment of need.

This is why I charge You with being missing during trouble, when Your Word says You will be present; I further charge you with leaving and forsaking, when your Word says You won't.

That's all I have, and frankly I see nothing You can say that can prove me wrong.

I rest my case.

I'm not the first to put Jesus on trial, of course. He has faced plenty of accusations, demands, and even taunting from people for Him to prove that He is God, from the devil tempting him in the desert to soldiers, prisoners, and others taunting him as He hung on the cross that He should save Himself, if He truly is who He claims to be.

My charge of God's abandonment, however, is not about taunting Him; my challenges are all about trust. If this relationship thing is real, if God's Word is true, than either He had a reason for not showing up or I am seriously missing something. I am not sure how God will respond, but nothing else matters to me right now; my faith, ministry, career path, and livelihood are all at risk. After all, how can I tell others about trusting God when I am not sure I can trust Him?

So I wait to hear His defense to my charges.

That is, if He decides to answer me this time.

CHAPTER 18

THE HEDGE

Well, God chooses to answer all right. In fact, it isn't long before I am shocked by the live witnesses He brings right into my hospital room.

Jesus: If it pleases the court—in other words, prosecutor, judge, and jury Kevin Ramsby—I'd like to call your wife Sarah as a witness.

Sarah notices I am caught off guard by the appearance of my hands; wrapped up mummy-like, they better resemble clubs than anything with fingers. So she begins helping me understand what happened to them.

"When you came in, your left pinky finger and right thumb had been badly hurt. All of the tendons and nerves were cut, and you couldn't move them at all," she explains. "After the first surgery, they needed to take you back in for more surgery on the second day to deal with your hands. They asked me what I thought— should they attempt to fix them or because they were in such bad shape, should they let your hands go so you wouldn't have to undergo more surgery."

This is the first time I've heard that; I can't believe God allowed such weighty decisions to be put upon Sarah.

"I just don't get it," I tell her. "Where was God in all this? On the ground praying, I had such a strong belief that God would show up or reveal

Himself in some way. But He didn't. Was He surprised by this, like me?" I am not bitter so much as disoriented. Seriously—why wasn't He there? He should have been. How can I trust a God who seemingly picks and chooses when He has to do what He said He would do?

I guess I expect Sarah to be sympathetic, understanding, and jumping on my bandwagon of doubt and disbelief. But God knows better; I don't realize it at the time, but this conversation is a set-up orchestrated by the Lord, who knew what He was doing when He put Sarah by my side. Sarah doesn't answer right away, but when she does, she shows herself to be a key witness for the defense.

"You know what, Kevin? I don't think He was surprised," she finally says. "I think He was looking out for you. For us. Think about it—we were all supposed to be home that night. The two weeks of the kids staying in Illinois was over, and they were supposed to have come home during the daytime on that day. Remember? We changed their plans just twenty-four hours before all this happened, since you were supposed to be out of town that week for the church-planting conference."

Sarah's voice is soft—half from compassion, half from the hush of what could have been. I can also tell my wife is a little nervous about whether she is crossing some emotional boundary; she is sure about her points, but she's also very aware of the fact that she was not there and has no idea what my life was like in those brutal minutes.

"I am so sorry this happened to you, but I think you're wrong," she continues gently. "I believe God *was* aware that something was going to happen, and He led us to change our plans. My heart breaks that this happened to you, but He protected the kids. He made sure we would not be there, because who knows what would have happened then?"

Jesus: Thank you Sarah. Your witness.

I am silent, though; realizing my wife has a valid point, I find myself thinking through an entirely different line of questioning.

What could have happened to Sarah and the kids if they'd been home that night? What if I couldn't defend them any more than I could myself? What harsh realities of life could my kids have seen with their still-innocent eyes? I hope they would have hidden, but even if they had, what screams, yells, and horror was my family rescued from in the sudden changing of plans?

I begin to see that all of my attention and focus has been on my hurts. My pain. My brokenness. Through Sarah, God began to show me that it is my too-narrow perspective, centered only upon what happened and how it hurt, that could be hiding His faithfulness. Could it be that maybe—just maybe—God's presence is best seen in what is left intact or untouched rather than what was allowed?

After all, even the Bible's Job—a guy who knew a thing or two about allowed wrongs and tremendous hurt—experienced a certain hedge of protection.

Remember, God—who never *authors* harm, but sometimes *authorizes* it—allowed the devil to test Job's faith by using people and what we consider today to be acts of God in nature to steal, kill, and destroy Job's children, livestock, and servants. But even in this, one of the Bible's greatest real-life examples of suffering, the hurts allowed were not limitless; God didn't allow Satan to take Job's wife, for example, or his life. He didn't allow Satan to prevent Job from being blessed with second chances at family and fortune.

When Sarah presented her view, I began to realize that like with Job, God protected my life and wife; I even got to keep my kids, and all my attacker got from the house, I'd come to find out, was an old laptop and a few dollars from my daughter's piggy bank (he never did find the keys to my Excursion). And while I didn't know what lay ahead, I did know that from the moment I'd heard "they still need you," I'd had a miraculous second chance.

But honestly, that only goes so far in for me in this moment. See, that's not what I asked for, and God knows it.

When I was lying there bleeding and hopeless, I wanted a *sign* from Him, something that assured me of His presence. I mean, in the Bible God communicated to people through His Word, writing on a wall, a star, animals, visions, dreams, and many times through angels. So I expected to see an angel, get a comforting word of scripture like Sarah herself got in Psalm 18:17-19, or get a vision of heaven or lights.

Sarah, by the way, is still grateful I didn't get all that. "You did *not* need to be walking toward any light!" she points out to this day. Nonetheless, I just didn't think it was too much to ask for the Creator of the universe to make His nearness known when and how I asked. So I'm not letting God off the hook easily.

Fortunately, Jesus isn't the combative defense attorney you might expect from a God accused of abandonment by someone for whom He died. The ultimate wise and experienced Defender is never shaken by my accusations or heartfelt questions. Knowing the depth of my pain, He is only concerned with truth and justice.

Jesus: I'd like to call my next witnesses: the detectives investigating the attack, and the medical team from the night of the attack.

CHAPTER 19
DIVINE APPOINTMENTS

In the early days in the hospital, the doctors don't know how long my recovery will be, nor the extent to which I will recover.

"One thing I do know," the chief surgeon tells me, "is you will never be able to do sit ups after this. Your stomach muscles looked like hamburger meat when we got you; we put them back together, but they are no longer normal."

My mind zeroes in on that word, normal. How can anything be normal for me after this? The happy anticipation of just a few days ago seems like a different life. So much for the citywide sports program for kids. So much for heading up a Revival Tabernacle church plant. Can *this* be my life? Are my dreams as ruined as my hands?

Then, there's the whole spiritual void. Trying to read my Bible for the first time since the attack lasts a full twenty seconds. It bothers me, but I quickly find I have no desire to read the Bible, to pray, or to hear from God. That's not normal, for me.

Even as I try to shut down hearing from Him, though, the Great Defender is able to sneak up on me.

It starts with the interviews with the detectives, who make me recount every detail of that night multiple times. Each time I walk them

through what happened, one of the detectives comments about a fact that grabs my attention as it relates to God's alleged abandonment of me.

"So what made you get up and go downstairs?" a detective asks. "Did you hear the guy or something else?" To me, this seems like a silly thing to question. The loud, startling shatter of glass breaking sounded as if someone only feet away threw a glass as hard as they could onto the ground right beside me. Who wouldn't wake to that? To the detectives, though, it is worth questioning.

"When we walked into your room, your TV was blaring and your noisy window air conditioner next hard, we don't know how in the to your bed was blowing so world you could hear glass breaking from a second-floor bedroom while sleeping. Talk about luck," one says.

Now keep in mind, these guys aren't hunting for God, they are fact finders bent on noting only the evidence they saw. But the more they speak, the more I can't help hearing them as unbiased witnesses for God, sharing small details that produced a big result: my survival.

For example, the detectives are amazed my neighbor was awake and available after 3 a.m. when I got to the top of his porch steps that August night.

"Your neighbor had just gotten off work; he went into his home just minutes before you showed up on his porch," they tell me. "That's why you didn't have to ring the door bell, and he was right there to call 911."

"He was definitely in the right place at the right time on that night."

That phrase, "in the right place at the right time," definitely gets my attention. In church, I've used that phrase many times to describe "divine appointments"—occasions where God directs people to be in a particular place at the exact time needed for a life- intersecting moment. So to hear matter-of-fact detectives talking all churchy does the same thing that Sarah sharing a different perspective had; I start to think about what might have happened if my neighbor hadn't gotten home minutes before I needed him.

Would he have heard me knocking? How long would that have taken? What would have happened if I'd had to go to another home? Every second mattered, as I was already beginning to slip in and out of consciousness. Would I have made it? Or might I have collapsed in a yard, only to be found dead the next day?

God isn't done using the detectives as defense witnesses, either. That becomes clear when they share the police's response time that night.

"It took less than ninety seconds for the police to show up at the home," they tell me.

"Are you kidding me?" I ask. Anyone familiar with living in a populous inner city knows a response time of ninety seconds is about as likely as the Detroit Lions making the playoffs. I remember calling the police years ago when a man, showed up at church wielding a large knife. (What's the deal with me and guys with knives?) I'd had to call 911 just like my neighbor had. And it was ninety *minutes* before a patrol car nonchalantly pulled up. The night of the attack, though, the response time was a-minute-and-a- half, as police officers were right around the block.

So again, I can't help but think about what could have happened if they hadn't been. Would my attacker—who, I will find out later, saw me on my neighbor's porch from my upstairs window—have come over and finished me off if he hadn't heard approaching sirens?

The neighbor and the police officers weren't the only ones in the right place at the right time, either. Through the stream of doctors and nurses who start popping into my room—many just to check in because they'd been there the night I arrived and were moved by the trauma—I learn how remarkable the staffing at the hospital was the night of the attack.

Rarely is a top surgeon and specialist present at this hospital after 3 a.m. The night I was attacked, however, the surgeon who performed my life-saving surgery was not at home on call, but in the building when I arrived. So were the other members of the team. Not having to wait for people to arrive saved minutes when minutes mattered most. Whose hand do you suppose pushed the paramedics toward the hospital that had such a remarkable medical team ready and waiting?

Could it have been the same hand that lined up just the right people in the right place at the right time for the Old Testament's Ruth?

Ruth had lost her husband, so she needed to navigate life post- trauma. At a crossroads of trusting and doubting, the young widow chose to forgo the seemingly easier road of returning home to her own family to instead be faithful to God in following her also- grieving mother-in-law Naomi to an unknown land.

Survival meant Ruth couldn't just stay locked in her room; she had to begin moving forward. She had to fight through feelings to make choices based on responsibility: eat or die. So she pushed past her painful past and uncertain future to engage fully in the day in front of her, heading out to pick up the leftover grain behind anyone who would let her.

It was an ordinary day. The second chapter of the book of Ruth reports no sign, voice, vision, or goose-bump moment from God.

But *as it turned out,* as the Bible puts it in Ruth 2:3, she found herself working a field belonging to a man named Boaz. It goes on to say *just then* Boaz returned from a trip and stopped by to greet the harvesters. His eyes were drawn to a woman he never had seen before in his fields; he asked about her, and was touched by her story. He made sure she was protected and treated kindly, provided food and water during the day and made arrangements, when she was not looking, for his men to deliberately leave stalks behind for her to pick up.

That's a lot of favor, right? But God didn't stop there. It turned out Boaz was a relative on Naomi's husband's side. This divine appointment was no small thing, since family was supposed to take care of family in the custom of the day.

The rest is history. Boaz ended up marrying Ruth, and the two became the parents of a son named Obed, the grandparents of a boy named Jesse, and the great-grandparents of David whose family line continued on to Jesus, who would take our punishment when He died on the cross for the sins of humanity.

No small thing, indeed.

As for me, I'm starting to have some regrets about bringing this charge against God. Maybe my feelings may have been getting the better of me and drowning out a reality the defense is beginning to show me with His witnesses. Could my allegations have been unfair? Could I be the one who failed to see something?

Jesus, though, isn't done showing me what He has to show me. He knows how much He was there. How much He cared. And He wants me to know it too.

Perhaps that's why He called me to the stand last.

CHAPTER 20

FINGERPRINTS OF GOD

Like any good defender, Jesus doesn't present the evidence of His presence the night of the attack in one fell swoop, where it might be easy to overlook the fine points. Instead, He lets it reach me bit by bit in the midst of my spiritual numbness.

Replaying events in my mind me, really; as I go over and noticing several parts of the is like Jesus' cross-examination of over what happened, I can't help ordeal becoming more and more challenging to my case that He had abandoned me.

Jesus: Kevin, what do you make of the knife?

I've thought so much about the knife and that moment where I was suddenly, shockingly holding it in the middle of the fight. In the early days in the hospital, I learned it actually broke—that's how I came to grab the blade, not the handle. Knifes do sometimes break in violent stabbings. But it is *how* this knife broke—not hitting a solid object, but *in midair,* my hand grabbing the blade without it hitting the ground—that is bizarre. That wasn't just divine, it was life-preserving; if the knife had stayed in its original condition, the twenty to twenty-five stabs I endured past that point probably would have killed me.

Jesus: Thank you, Kevin. And how do you suppose you went from being unable to move to standing up?

Yeah, I'm still amazed by that. After those agonizing stabs to the back of the neck, I'd been unable to turn over, much less get up— so how did I stand to my feet and get out of my home? I flat-out can't explain it without crediting the hand of God.

Jesus: Thank you, Kevin. Next, can you explain hearing the words, "they still need you?"

Well, I couldn't have thought the words up right then. First, only death was on my mind; all strength, hope, and possibility had been depleted in the fight. Plus, my thoughts were occupied with praying for Noah at the time; those four startling words had to *interrupt* me to get my attention. And no one was anywhere near me to speak them—no one human, anyway. Yet those words were so real, so clear.

Come to think of it, the four words I heard were kind of like a personalized form of one of the most common messages from God to His people in the Bible: essentially, get up. In 1 Kings 19:5-7, an angel twice touched Elijah and said "get up" in the prophet's weakest moments. In Acts 8:26 (KJV), Philip heard the words "Arise, and go," which initiated a change in direction and led him to a divine appointment with an Ethiopian eunuch who was stuck in his spiritual journey. In Matthew 2:13, Jesus' earthly dad Joseph was told to "get up" and "escape" in his life-or-death moment when his family was being hunted by Herod.

Could "they still need you" have been my "get up" moment, made more personal to me by a very-present God who knew "get up" wouldn't have been enough? See, I was convinced I *couldn't* get up; the words "they still need you" were probably the only words that could get me to act immediately despite everything that was taking place.

It is hard to remember hearing those words and hold the line that God abandoned me.

Jesus: Thank you, Kevin. And can you share what you have been hearing from the doctors about the wounds you received?

Well, basically, that for me to survive such a vicious attack was a miracle.

Dr. Renny, our family friend who was on the scene in those early days, said mine was by far the worst stabbing case he's ever seen. Yet despite thirty-seven wounds, *not one* vital organ was damaged critically. The three that were hit at all were only nicked and easily repaired. There were tons of near-misses—if one to the temple had been slightly lower, I would have lost an eye, if the two in my throat had been slightly deeper, my jugular could have been pierced, and I most definitely would have bled out quickly—but no fatal blows.

"Just looking at the odds of something like this happening and not doing more damage or resulting in a fatality—I can't explain it," Dr. Renny would later say. "In my book, this is a miracle."

Did you say Dr. Renny called it a miracle? Jesus double-checks. *Okay, thank you. Kevin, can you think of any other times the Father revealed His presence in "how do you explain that?" ways?*

Well, Biblically, you can see God's fingerprints in the fact that the Israelites' sandals never wore out after leaving Egypt, though they wandered forty years in the wilderness—not exactly home to a Payless on every corner. His fingerprints are there in the widow's oil that never went out in the Old Testament, and the feeding of the 5,000 with a few loaves of bread and a handful of fish in the New Testament.

Jesus: Thank you, Kevin. You have been most helpful. I have just one more question, about what Aaron witnessed in the house.

Aaron—our youth pastor who became Sarah's representative to receive information at the hospital until she got there—also was one of the first "unofficial" personnel allowed to enter the house after the attack.

He told me he'll probably never forget the pool of blood on the floor, nor the blood streaks that ran down the wall; his horror echoed that of the responding officers, who later revealed they never had seen anything as graphic as the scene at 110 Montana after that fateful battle.

"Listen, probably the thing that baffles me the most," Aaron said, "is we see where you lost consciousness, we see the huge pool of blood, we see how it overflowed and filled the whole first two steps where you went down to get out of the house. We saw how you stood up in the blood, where you had to use the walls to balance yourself."

"But we don't know how you got from your kitchen to your neighbor's porch. Even though you stood up *in the blood*, there's no footprints, no drops, nothing."

Mind you, I'd put my feet into the pool of blood to stand up, and I'd still been so drenched in blood by the time I got to my neighbor's porch that the cops couldn't tell what race I was, and the paramedics struggled to get my slippery body onto a gurney.

Yet—no bloody footprints.

Jesus: So that's what Aaron saw; I'd also like to submit the police reports that detail the crime scene and also report no such blood evidence from the top of the steps to the neighbor's porch. Can you explain that, Kevin?

I can't—not without divine intervention, anyway.

I am beginning to see the light; clearly, Jesus is teaching me that sometimes God's presence is best seen by what cannot be explained. My footprints may not have been on the bloody scene, but God's fingerprints were all over it.

In fact, it looks a lot like when I thought God was the farthest from me, He was actually the closest to me.

CHAPTER 21
THE VERDICT

So the verdict is in: God has proven Himself innocent of abandonment. Showing me the hedge around my family, the divine appointments, and the unusual details that point to the fingerprints of God, Jesus broke through to me while I was on spiritual life- support. He showed me God had lived up to His Word in Psalm 46:1 and Deuteronomy 31:6, the very verses I'd hurled at Him; I had to concede He hadn't left me, He hadn't abandoned me, and He *had* been my ever present help in time of need.

In fact, if He hadn't been there, I wouldn't be here.

Ironically, accusing God of abandonment in a trial that was supposed to prove His distance from me gave me a new sense of closeness to and connection with Him. Having accused God of abandonment, I now relate to Jesus when He cried out on the cross, "My God, my God, why have you forsaken me?" It comforts me that the One I accused knows what it feels like in the moment of seeming betrayal, that He's been there.

What Jesus taught me through the trial reminds me of the epic story of Shadrach, Meshach, and Abednego in Daniel 3. Not unlike a certain pastor just faithfully typing in some information about ministry, watching a little TV, then slipping off to sleep on a regular August night, these guys were just living their lives— handling some local affairs in Babylon and worshiping God.

Suddenly some random astrologers got the word out that our heroes were having the audacity to refuse to worship false idols that King Nebuchadnezzar had set up, and Shadrach, Meshach, and Abednego were threatened with getting tossed in a blazing furnace because of it.

"Then what god will be able to rescue you from my hand?" Nebuchadnezzar demanded when he ordered them to worship his little figures in Daniel 3:15.

Famously, Shadrach, Meshach, and Abednego responded with some of the most faith-filled words of the Old Testament; essentially: "Okay, no problem. God is able to rescue us from some little fire. P.S."—and here's where their faith gets a little crazy—"even if he does not, He's still our God, not you or your images of gold and whatnot." So: off to the fire with them.

But it didn't end there. Nebuchadnezzar himself witnessed what happened next.

"Weren't there three men that we tied up and threw in the fire?...Look! I see four men walking around in the fire, unbound and unharmed, and the fourth looks like a son of the gods," he asked in Daniel 3:24, probably freaking out a good bit. We know who that fourth was, of course. So Nebuchadnezzar pulled the other three out as quickly as he could. (Wouldn't you?)

Jesus has shown me so much about this story, as he Has much else in the Bible, in light of what happened in August 2009:

- I wasn't left alone any more than Shadrach, Meshach, and Abednego were.

- God's presence actually became stronger *in* the fire; notice the three men didn't see God *before* being thrown into the furnace, nor *after* they were rescued. God showed up when they needed Him most.

- God can protect a person in the fire. I *was* protected physically, as funny as that may sound coming from a guy stabbed more than three dozen times. God may not have delivered me from the fire, any more than he did Shadrach, Meshach, and Abednego, but He certainly brought me through it alive and remarkably functional, really.

- Finally, sometimes, it takes someone standing outside the fire to see the extra presence in the fire. When he told me about the lack of bloody footprints, Aaron was the witness standing outside my fire who figuratively jumped up and said look! Look! There's Someone Else there!

Okay, so God didn't visibly show Himself in the form of an angel or through some lights the night of the stabbing. But He didn't ignore my prayer that He come to me, He just answered it differently than I expected. Through the trial, I'd learned sometimes it's better to have God *not* do the one thing you want because He's busy doing the fifty other things He knows you need.

Some called the details surrounding my survival miracles, and others called them luck. As for me, I continue to be completely floored by the fact this uninvited wrong would have been deadly if it weren't for the "but God" factor. It's how I started to see I needed to take some cues from the Old Testament's Joseph, who made room for God to turn things around when he told his brothers and wrongdoers, "You intended to harm me, *but God* intended it for good..." in Genesis 50:20. What a cool idea, that God might use what was intended for evil for good. It was exciting, starting to think about Him doing that in my life.

Through putting God on trial, I learned that even the sense of being abandoned doesn't actually indicate being out of God's will or presence. I also learned that allowing God to come close to wrongs and wounds and show me how to keep trusting Him helped even more than revealing the wrongs or acknowledging the hurts. It was exactly what I needed, not only to begin healing, but to begin fighting again.

You see, even when the trial of God was over, I wasn't done having to fight, not by a long shot. In fact, the biggest fight—the one upon which getting to discover God's greater purposes absolutely hinged—was yet to begin. Fortunately, I was able to enter it secure in the idea that no matter what my perceptions might become when I get overwhelmed or struggle, Jesus wouldn't ever leave my side.

Good thing, because He was about to drop the ultimate F bomb in my heart: forgiveness.

LET'S GET READY TO RUMBLE!

When I initially relived the attack over and over, my mind zipped through and past my attacker without much attention; when I was zeroing in on God's supposed abandonment of me, I sort of dismissed my attacker's part of what happened as being due to broken, sinful, fallen humanity.

That wouldn't last, though.

It is on a Wednesday, more than a full week after the attack, when my focus starts to shift toward the man who had wielded the knife. I am still in the hospital, my mind unable to stop hearing and reflecting on the words, "they still need you."

Who are "they"? Who needs me? Is it just Noah and Caitlin and Sarah? Or could there be others out there who also need me?

It isn't long before those questions lead to me thinking, for the first time, what life will look like beyond the hospital—more specifically, what will become of me. I've spent years working with casualties of life, so I know firsthand how often people who have been traumatized or hurt by others end up spending the rest of their lives fighting an uphill battle where a new normal is never regained. Now, it's my turn in life's hot seat, and I have to wonder: Will I become bitter or better? Will this thick fog and haze of hurt limit my ability to see those around me? What would it take for me to actually be useful—mentally and emotionally present rather than stuck in the past—to whoever needs me?

Oh man.

I am going to have to deal with the forgiveness thing.

Forgiveness comes up like something beginning to press in on me. Something irritating, the way a pebble is in your shoe—distracting and very uncomfortable. I begin to hear a new question pushing to get my attention; I try not to hear it, but it's as relentless as my attacker was.

"What are you going to do with this man?"

It was like God put me in a boxing ring under pressure to get up after a knock-down punch, and the key to rising before the count of ten was answering that question.

"What are you going to do with this man?"

One.

Wait a minute.

Two.

How can I forgive this guy? I don't even know where to begin!

Three.

Seriously? He is still out on the loose, for heaven's sake. What if he's not even sorry?

Four.

You understand that because of this guy, I'm living with an intense, constant, exhausting fear, right?

Five.

Hold ON. How do I forgive when I'm still so angry?

Six.

Please! Just wait! How can I "forgive and forget" when I remember every second?

Seven.

This is too much! I'm stuck. I just can't let it go. How do I move forward?

Eight.

So if I forgive, then what? Do I ever get any actual closure?

NINE ...

All right. All right! I give up—fine. I'll choose forgiveness.

Sounds great, right? Noble, godly, scriptural, and most importantly, final. But here's the thing: though I say the three big words, "I will forgive," nothing changes in me. My doubts, hurt, memories, feelings, and questions are the same as they were just a few seconds before choosing forgiveness.

Still, for the first time since this mess began, I'm calling the shots. That part, at least, feels good; Sarah was right on when she wrote in her journal that I'm a fighter and I want to get better. By choosing to forgive, I'm also choosing to fight for freedom from all those things trying to keep me a prisoner of the attack: seeing myself from a victim's perspective, fear, bitterness, relentless flashbacks of what happened, and what words to choose if and when the day comes when I get to confront my attacker and seek closure.

Now I just have to find out *how* to fight. This will be no easy feat; I'll go five bloody rounds with the obstacles and enemies that stand between me and victory, and each round is much longer, more grueling and more complicated than the literal fight on the night of the attack, or wrestling with God after. That said, each round is very much worth fighting, as they will determine whether I can finish making space for God to do a work in and through me, or will stay trapped and damaged for the rest of my life.

So, in the words of the famous boxing announcer, "*Let's get ready to rumble!*"

PART FOUR

LETTING IT GO

FIGHTING TO FORGIVE

CHAPTER 22

ROUND 1: PERSPECTIVE

"Kevin?" The doctor's voice shakes me out of my private thoughts. "How are you feeling?"

"Pretty good," I tell him with a tired smile.

"Oh good, then you're ready," he says.

It's only been a few days since God dropped the forgiveness bomb, and now it's time to begin the painful process of getting back up on my feet. If I don't, I'll be at risk of blood clots, pneumonia, and painful sores that would create greater complications and delay recovery, so I'm good with the idea of walking. I just hope I can do it.

Then, the doctor lowers the boom.

"We need to get you up and walking so we can get you out of here and back home in the next day or two."

What? I think. *I'm supposed to go where? And when???* The doctor went on to explain the hospital actually isn't the best environment for me to continue healing, due to the high risk of infection for the wounds left open to heal from the inside out—a fitting metaphor for what would need to happen to my mind and spirit, though I don't notice that at the time. I'm fixated on one word: home. *Where's home?* So as soon as the doctor finishes up and walks out of earshot, I unleash the sheer panic inside me to my wife.

"Sarah, what are we going to do? I can't return to Montana Street. I'm sorry, I just can't. What if he comes back? I can't fight or defend you or the kids," I tell her, my heart pounding at the thought. "I'm just not ready."

I see the surprise about my reaction in Sarah's eyes, but as usual she remains strong for me.

"It's going to be okay, babe. We are going to be fine. Let's just talk about it and think it through," she says calmly. I quickly begin hard selling her on a hotel, though Sarah doesn't take much convincing; she just wants me to get and be well.

So after one more day—and, rather astonishingly, after just two weeks total—we leave the safety and comfort of Henry Ford Hospital for what will be a two-week stint in a hotel.

The time in the hotel is incredibly busy for Sarah; she no longer has the kids off on playdates all the time or hospital staff caring for me. So she manages two kids bouncing off the walls, oversees my wound care twice a day, and helps shower, shave, dress, and feed me, along with beginning to take care of things like the bills, arranging for the kids to start in a new school, and making decisions about repairing our home.

My inability to do much physically has an interesting side effect; I become much more tuned in to what Sarah is doing than I usually am when both of us are busy. I also become overwhelmed by gratitude for the many, many other loved ones who came to my side or reached out to me through this time, and I begin to see a connection between the love being shown me and this seemingly impossible task to make forgiveness anything more than a few cheap words.

See, while my family and friends all say the words, "We love you Kevin," it's their actions toward me that turn the word "love" into an experiential reality. 1 Corinthians 13 is so true when it says, love *is,* for genuine, authentic, biblical love always involves action and effort. So as I watch my wife, family, and friends put love in action, it doesn't take much to realize that forgiveness requires action and effort beyond words too.

But that's easier to recognize than to act on.

The reality is that forgiveness is very complex, and so difficult. As a Christ-follower, I get that I'm supposed to forgive, to let go of the offense and hurt. But as the victim of a terrible crime, I can barely focus on what I'm "supposed" to do in my growing passion to see the person who wronged me arrested, handcuffed, remorseful, humbled, broken. He messed up big time, and I don't care about his inability to right his wrongs; I want answers, then hard consequences. In other words, I'm not exactly coming from the best perspective to begin fighting to forgive, and frankly, I don't even know where to begin.

I know who does, though. So once again, I pray.

God, will you help me to forgive? My kids, my family, and others need me to come out of this fight standing as a victor and not a victim. How do I begin? I want to glorify You, and I long for my reactions to point others to You. Whatever it takes, I will choose forgiveness!

You might think God wouldn't begin to answer that prayer with Scripture, what with me having pushed my Bible away from me in the hospital. But the thing about the Bible is once you've spent time in it, the living, breathing word of God is accessible even if you're refusing to crack open the book itself. So after I pray, God starts bringing to my mind certain Scripture passages in light of this bout to forgive.

For example, Matthew 18:21-35. In this passage, a king forgives a huge debt a servant owed him, and I mean *huge*—some scholars say it would be the equivalent of tens of millions of dollars today. *Okay,* I think. *I should identify with this king in light of forgiveness where someone owes him so much and he cancels the debt the servant can't possibly make right.* I find it especially easy to relate when I read commentaries by people who believe this servant may have been stealing from the king; I know what it's like to be a victim of theft.

So why can't I stop zeroing in on the servant who owed the massive debt?

Why, with my thirty-seven stab wounds and useless hands, can't I shake this sense that I'm the debtor? This is just confusing in light of me needing to forgive someone who has wronged *me;* shouldn't the king be the one with whom I'm connecting? Needing a closer look to see how this scripture applies to my situation, I pick up my Bible for the first time since pushing it away in the hospital and begin examining Matthew 18.

As I read on, it quickly becomes apparent where God's going with this passage.

After being forgiven himself, the servant encountered a fellow servant who owed him way, way less than he himself had owed the king (more like a single day's wages as opposed to a fortune). Like the king, he had an opportunity to forgive a debt—but he didn't. Instead, he unleashed a shockingly violent attack, grabbing and choking the man who owed him and couldn't pay, then getting him thrown into prison like a criminal. So quick to forget his own guilt and the mercy and forgiveness he received, he became possessed by what was owed to him by another.

Then, it hits me like a ton of bricks.

The problem isn't how I see my attacker.

The problem is how I see myself.

I'm not focusing on the seventeen-year-old who called in bomb threats before encountering the pure love of God, or the thirty-seven-year-old who had a thought to check out Internet porn the morning of the attack. Despite the fact that I identify so much with the apostle Paul, who said in 1 Timothy 1:13-16 that he was once a "blasphemer, persecutor, and a violent man" and the worst of sinners who had been changed by the grace of God, I'm wanting mercy for me and mercilessness for my attacker.

But it doesn't work that way, God shows me; as Matthew 18 continues, when the king hears of his servant's injustice toward his own debtor, the ruler points out that the unforgiving servant should have shown mercy *just as* he'd experienced it himself. Since he didn't, he'd be sent to jail to experience torture after all.

Then comes the dagger.

"This is how my heavenly Father will treat each of you unless you forgive your brother or sister from your heart," Jesus tells the disciples in Matthew 18:35.

With that, four thoughts strike me as hard as any stab or punch I've ever received:

- Jesus said forgive "from your heart"—*man*. The heart is so much harder to change than your words, even than your actions. No wonder forgiveness is so difficult.

- It's crazy easy to forget how much and to what extent I've been forgiven by the King. Look how hard it was for me to even see why I was drawn toward the unforgiving servant! Clearly I am going to have to overcome my own tendency to forget that I've been forgiven, and forgiven much.

- Others' ability to make wrongs right or heal my hurts is irrelevant in the fight to forgive. In fact, Jesus wasn't focused on justice at all in this passage, just on unforgiveness. Here I'm thinking what will start to get me free is to see the person who wronged me arrested, handcuffed, and forced to stand before me in a court. But God's showing me it's my own remorse, accountability, humility, and brokenness that will head me in the direction.

- My forgiveness of others should look like and be "just and other as"—specifically, according to Colossians 3:1 and Ephesians 4:32, "just as" the Lord forgives me. In other words, it should be extended in the same way and manner as the great forgiveness granted to me by Jesus.

OK. So that's what God's trying to help me see with Matthew 18: I'm just like the guy who has forgotten how much he was forgiven because he got caught up in focusing on himself as the one who was owed something. As such, I see I'm at high risk for the consequence of unforgiveness: being tortured by my own emotions and obsessions.

That doesn't sound like the freedom for which I want to fight; it sounds like what I want freedom *from*, actually.

So clearly, my first opponent in the fight to forgive is my perspective of myself as the one who is owed something. Just as clearly, I need help fighting that trap by taking a closer look at exactly how Jesus did His forgiving so I can follow in His footsteps.

In other words, to gain perspective in the fight to forgive, I must revisit the cross.

CHAPTER 23

REVISITING THE CROSS

Having a relationship with Jesus gives me a major advantage in this fight for freedom from the perspective of being owed something. I have someone to look to, someone who can show me how it's done. C. H. Spurgeon put it this way: "If you want to learn about your need for forgiveness, go to the cross. If you want to learn about forgiving others, hang out there for a while."[v] So in my private moments when Sarah's buzzing around getting stuff done, I begin to see myself hanging out at Calvary.

I quickly find myself wondering how God could allow His beloved and only Son to be treated so unfairly and harshly.

I'm watching the only sinless and innocent man to walk this earth, Jesus, hanging naked, beaten, and on the verge of death. It's a dark day. The atmosphere is tense as those closest to the foot of the cross—the religious leaders, guards, and rulers—are all hollering at and ridiculing the dying Savior.

They are ruthless.

Every word, every demonic-like snarl of hatred and anger can be seen by the One who is willingly laying down His life for theirs. For ours. For mine.

---

[v] Greg Laurie, "Forgiven People," September 6, 2008, *Harvest Christian Fellowship* www.harvest.org (May 18, 2016)

I find myself staying at a distance. Closer, there is a group of women crying uncontrollably at the sight of Jesus; years earlier in my relationship with Christ, I would have been as devastated as they are. Now, things like having carried the title of pastor for fifteen years and my ministry accomplishments are more boast- worthy than my spiritual intimacy. So I'm more of an onlooker on this day, and find myself surrounded by others who also stay on the fringes of the crowd, wanting to be neither the attackers nor those who are hurting—as if, by taking notes and watching from a distance, we can be neutral.

I know the truth, though; there is no neutral ground with Jesus. You are either for or against. Plus, deep in my heart, despite my distance, I'm well aware of my pride, selfishness, jealousy, dishonesty, anger, lust, and other sins He is dying for.

Then in the midst of the chaos, heartache, emotional frenzy, mocking, and suffering, Jesus does something absolutely mind- boggling.

Jesus fights.

With death inching its way closer every second, Jesus can no longer keep quiet; He has to speak His heart, and He won't operate from a victim's perspective on this cross He willingly chose to endure. Where most hurting people naturally hurt others, Jesus throws His knockout punch in a totally different direction.

"Father, forgive them, for they do not know what they are doing," Jesus said. About those directly responsible for hurting him.

Wow. In the midst of suffering and hurt, Jesus begins pursuing his wrongdoers with forgiveness. They are oblivious to the magnitude of hurt and pain being inflicted on Him, and that they're the ones doing it—as I have been, I realize. It's there, at the cross, that I'm shocked by that truth as I hear in my spirit, "Father, forgive Kevin, for he does not know what he is doing."

Oh man. He is not just dying for my sins generally, but for the very one I am struggling with today: unforgiveness.

Revisiting the cross to combat perspective just got *extremely* personal.

See, when I go to the cross and imagine Jesus fighting back with forgiveness, I begin to see my attacker as no worse than me, a guilty man whose sins murdered a holy God's sinless Son. The cross becomes the basis of forgiveness, the tool to help me overcome my own tendency to forget that I've been forgiven much; it reminds me that no matter what someone has done to me, it will never be worse than what I did to Him.

Hanging out at the cross also shows me the very specific fighting words Jesus used that become the basis for the fight talk I need to begin using myself.

He said: *Father, forgive them, for they do not know what they are doing.*

To use the same fighting words myself, I must pray: *Father, forgive my attacker, for this man has no idea what he has done.* And Jesus' powerful prayer begins to actually create the perspective shift, the necessary softening of heart, by providing some fairly simple initial responses I can use to answer the questions trying to get in the way of my forgiveness fight. *Why did that guy attack me? Is he sorry or remorseful?* (It doesn't matter because it didn't matter to Jesus on the cross, I can respond.) *Why should I be the one who initiates forgiveness to someone who, to be very frank, doesn't deserve it?* (Because I'm commanded to forgive *just as* Jesus forgave me; in other words, since He initiated forgiveness and pursued me while I was in the middle of my sin, I'm called to do the exact same for my attacker.)

Father, forgive him, for he has no idea what he has done.

So I discovered that the cross is like a Christian's secret weapon in the fight to forgive; it shows me how to enter the ring, and where— since this is hardly a one-time battle—I can return any time for encouragement and example when unforgiveness begins getting the upper hand. To this day, remembering I've experienced forgiveness at such a huge level changes forgiveness from being impossible to being a fairly simple response.

When I remember, that is.

This is some heavy stuff when you're badly wounded and living in a hotel room wondering if your attacker will return.

Hanging out at the cross is also a pretty good place to be when two Highland Park detectives arrive to share the progress made in my case; they are about to make "forgive *him*" a lot more personal.

They know who did this to me. His name is Percy;[vi] he is from Birmingham, Alabama.

"Did you catch him yet?" I ask them. "Please tell me you have him."

Not yet, but they will, they tell me.

[vi] Name has been changed.

"We have warrants out for him now," they assure me. "We are putting his face up on the news tonight with a reward for his arrest. We will find him. We have his fingerprints." It turns out my attacker was not new to violence; he had been in prison most of his adult life, so his prints were on file.

"But you don't know where he is at right now?" I ask, still worried he might be trying to find me; after all, I'm the only witness who can identify or testify against him.

"I'm sorry Kevin, we don't. We are on it, though. It is our top priority and we'll stay in touch with you the moment we find anything out."

And just like that, the detectives leave the hotel and I have a name to attach to the face I often see when I close my eyes, and to the attack, and to all the hurts.

Father, forgive . . .

Father, forgive Percy.

It's a victory, and there's a relief to move forward in fighting to forgive. I can't say, though, that it brought complete peace. I start thinking about how this guy has a history of hurting people; no wonder the police chief said he thought the crime scene looked like a jailhouse stabbing. *Man, this habitual offender could still be in the neighborhood, for all I know*; the thought grips my heart and zaps every ounce of fight from me.

So it's quickly apparent that while my most strategic weapon in this fight to forgive is revisiting the cross, it's not the only trick I'll need up my sleeve. Why? Because the perspective of myself as the one who is owed something is not the only opponent.

Fear is about to step into the ring.

Great. With our money for a hotel running out, Round 2 in the fight to forgive revs up just as we begin preparing to head back to 110 Montana Street.

CHAPTER 24

ROUND 2: FEAR

"You can put the gun down, Pastor Art." I say, grinning at my old friend. "Seriously. I think I'm okay; I'm calmer now that you are here. Thanks for showing up."

It's the night I'd been dreading: our first night back at Montana Street, just one month since I was stabbed viciously and left for dead. I anticipated the first night back might be difficult, especially with my attacker still on the run, so Sarah and I made arrangements to have Art and Shari Ledlie stay with us. Pastor Art, the pastor responsible for bringing us to Detroit twelve years earlier, is licensed to carry a gun for personal protection. This night, it's for my protection.

The day didn't start with panic and the brandishing of guns, nor any dire, grave sense of dread; actually, it had been a wonderful homecoming. After a preliminary visit to Montana Street with some trusted friends went surprisingly well, the fear I'd had in the hotel has been replaced by a desire to return home.

Then, when the actual move-back day came, we arrived to find streamers, cake, a large orange paper banner with handwritten messages from a youth group in the Chicago area, and so many friendly faces. Mayor Hubert Yopp was the first one to greet us; I was touched that my city, as well as so many church members, family, and friends, had turned out to show their support. There was no sense of the unspeakable violence that had taken place, just the sounds of laughter, joking, and the warmth of the community gathered at our home.

In the month since the attack, our church family raised money for $12,000 worth of taxes on and changes to our home ranging from a huge new flat-screen TV to motion lights and an alarm system, and seeing my wife and kids excited about everything was awesome. I badly needed to know that coming home was best for my family too, and with their reactions, I felt hope that everything might end up being okay. I was home, not returning to the scene of a crime.

Not yet, anyway.

As evening approached, the guests left, along with Noah and Caitlin, who were to stay at a church family's home. For the couple hours between everyone leaving and the Ledlies arriving, I found myself starting to panic. So I am relieved to finally have Pastor Art by my side around 9:30 p.m., especially when he immediately begins unzipping a black leather case concealing his .45 Sig Sauer Pistol and a .38 Smith & Wesson revolver.

The last time I saw Pastor Art packing heat, he was aiming at pigeons in a warehouse; now, he is all about protecting me and mine. And frankly, even though I'd told him it was okay to put his gun down—I've never been a big gun guy—I have to admit I feel a little safer with Pastor Art's arsenal at hand, especially considering how a tennis racket did the night of the attack.

"I'm not sure how this is going to go tonight," I tell Pastor Art as he flips open chambers to load bullets. "I'm feeling pretty nervous already, and I'm not too sure this is a good idea. I'm still scared he could know I'm back here and show up."

"Oh man, don't worry about that," my old friend replies. "I'm ready if he does." He flips the chamber back into place. "I've got your back, Kevmo."

So after my wife arms the newly installed security system, the four of us go upstairs. Sarah, exhausted from her two weeks of nonstop caretaking in the confines of a hotel room, is happy to settle into her first night in her own bed. As Shari settles into Caitlin's room, Pastor Art and I head to Noah's room, where my friend settles down into Noah's bed with his guns by his side while I settle down in a recliner nearby.

I'm exhausted, but too keyed up to relax; every ten minutes or so I'm checking my watch, desperately wanting the morning to come and getting more and more anxious. It's 11 p.m. before I can doze off at all. Every time I close my eyes and start to doze off, Pastor Art quietly gets up with his .38 Smith & Wesson revolver in hand and positions himself at the top of my steps. He watches. He listens for any unfamiliar sounds. He places himself in the middle of any danger that could threaten us.

That's how Pastor Art put his love into action.

Sleep doesn't last long; after just minutes, I wake with sweat pouring from my forehead, my hands trying (despite being bandaged to splints) to grip the arm rests, and my eyes bulging like a mad man as I relive the attack in my mind. So Pastor Art quickly returns to the room to reassure me.

"I'm here, Kevmo. It's okay," he says. "Nothing is happening." Nonetheless, that cycle happens again and again, so after a while, I give up, substituting bits of sleep for episodes of *Everybody Loves Raymond*. Not that it distracts me much; I'm getting more uptight at every tick of the clock as it moves closer to 3 a.m., the time I was awakened by breaking glass the last night I'd spent at home.

When the clock moves past 3 a.m., however, I start to relax. *Maybe it is going to be okay,* I think.

Then suddenly the lights around us and the TV suddenly flip off, and in an instant, I'm just as terrified as I was a month ago.

He cut the power! He is back! He cut the power! He is back! My stomach drops and my heart is in my throat as my mind races to my worst nightmare becoming a reality.

"Pastor Art, quick, get up! He's back, he's back. Pastor Art, he's here!" I say, and Pastor Art jumps to his feet and scrambles to pull out his guns; *click click* I hear in the midst of the kind of intense adrenaline high I'd experienced only once before. With my pounding pulse masking both the ability to think clearly and the pain from my stomach wounds, I instinctively jump from my recliner and rush the best I can toward Sarah in our room as Pastor Art races down the stairs.

"Get up, Sarah, get up—he's back!" I burst into our bedroom yelling. "Get out the window, hurry, he's back!"

"What? What are you talking about?" she mutters sleepily.

"Come on, he's here," I say urgently. "Get up and get out the window!"

Sarah sighs heavily; she's neither panicked nor particularly cooperative. "Why is Pastor Art running down the stairs?" she asks. "Didn't we learn last time this isn't a good idea?" That throws me. What should I do? Pastor Art is racing downstairs, maybe into harm's way, and my wife is refusing to get up.

"Sarah, GET UP! He's back, you have to get away!"

My wife flops over. "Well, he can just kill me then because I'm too tired. I'm not going anywhere."

What??? How is Sarah so indifferent to the situation? I know she wasn't there that night, but I don't understand why she isn't trusting and listening to me. I can't do anything more though, so I pause and listen for sounds downstairs.

"Pastor Art. Pastor Art. You okay? What's going on?" My heart was racing a million miles an hour, and my knees were trembling so violently I could hardly stay standing.

Silence.

"Pastor Art? What's going on? Come on dude, what's up?"

Then thankfully, a response.

"Everything is okay," he said; I heard him begin to walk up the dark stairwell, guns still in hand. "Everything is fine so far. No one is here."

"What's going on, guys?" I heard Sarah say; she was finally beginning to get out of her bed, and Shari was coming out of Caitlin's room.

"The power went out. I think he cut the power and is back," I said, breathing hard. "Where's my phone? I'm calling the police." As I hit the button for the direct number to the police, which was already programmed into my phone for a moment like this, I began thinking of barricading myself in our bedroom, giving no thought to Pastor Art and Shari who would be left to fend for themselves outside the door. Looking back, I feel so selfish, but in the moment, all sense was muted by sheer panic.

Meanwhile, I get hold of an officer on duty at the Highland Park police station just one-and-a-half miles from my house.

"This is Pastor Kevin from Revival Tabernacle, the pastor who was stabbed in the home invasion a month ago. I think the guy is back and trying to get into my house. I think he cut the power to the house. I have a guy here with a gun but need someone to get here right away. Hurry, he's back, he's . . ."

But the officer interrupts.

"Pastor, it's okay! It's okay. You are going to be fine. Trust me, you're safe. A four-block area in your neighborhood just lost its power a few minutes ago. Something blew, and they are already on it and beginning to fix it."

My heart rate slowly begins to calm down.

"Are you sure?" I ask.

"Yes," he says. "It's not just your home."

"Okay then." I can feel my legs back under me; the tingling and rubbery feeling is subsiding. "Please send someone to check though, I'm just not sure." Within minutes, I see two police officers arrive, but I still jump when the doorbell rings. The three officers on the porch explain they had already walked around my entire house and driven up and down the alley shining the spotlight between houses and on the abandoned homes on my block; they assure me everything is okay.

Okay.

Okay. Now, there is nothing left to do but finish calming down. It takes a while, but eventually, I settle back into my recliner. Sleep is out of the question, of course; Pastor Art and I are now wide awake, despite it being around 4:15 a.m.

So the TV is back on as soon as the power returns.

Then, suddenly I hear another commotion outside my window.

"Shh. Shh." I mute the TV quickly. "Do you hear that Pastor Art?" Someone is out front, yelling.

"This is crazy," I whisper, turning the TV off to darken the room as we both get up. I walk over to the window and peek outside while listening to the *click click* as Pastor Art takes out the .45 Sig Sauer.

"There are people outside," I said. "What's going on, can you see?" Pastor Art begins separating another set of blinds to look.

"There are two people. Looks like they are kind of arguing," he says.

Wait. Maybe this had nothing to do with the attacker; there is a tow truck out there, and I can identify one of the guys raising his voice. It is my neighbor, the one who called 911 for me.

"I think they are trying to take his car or something," I tell Pastor Art. "It looks like it's a repossession." I think back to how my neighbor had been up when I pounded on his door this time a month ago; I wondered if the repo guy had been waiting for him tonight to get off work.

A few minutes pass, and everything settles down. The tow truck drives off, and the night finally gives way to calmness.

Whew. "This has been an absolutely crazy night," I say as we both make our way back to the room to try to get a bit of rest.

It is the first of what will be many, many nights with barely a lick of sleep. When I get up to start the next day, the physical exhaustion is nothing compared to the mental exhaustion; I am just wrecked. I feel like I've just finished a brutal, fifteen-round boxing match.

Because I have.

You know how God puts just the right people and elements in play at just the right times to accomplish His plans? The morning after that crazy, dramatic night, I realize I'm seeing that the Enemy works in a similar fashion. Think about it: the first night back in this house, at nearly the exact time of the attack, a small number of homes lose power—and ours is one of them. I don't think that was a coincidence, nor was the noisy commotion shortly thereafter.

Instead, I believe it was the opening bell announcing an opponent named fear.

CHAPTER 25

RELEASING FEAR

Fear is such a common opponent it's almost easy to dismiss it— and that's part of its trickery. It's incredibly strategic and intentional, and a bully rather than a knock-out artist, designed to wear us down physically, mentally, and spiritually. Creating exhaustion by provoking a life lived on defense, it uses sharp jabs to try to get us to come to unreasonable conclusions, and it cripples the strongest of fighters with its uncanny ability to cause a person to lose sight of the Victor.

That's what it did to the prophet Elijah.

Elijah was one of the greatest fighters of all time. Bold, courageous, trusting in God and confident in his faith, he stood toe-to-toe with some formidable threats in his day, and for the longest time, he fought them with spiritual weapons and won.

Until he didn't.

Elijah's fighting instincts and skills are unleashed, and God's trustworthy presence is fully seen, in 1 Kings 17 and 18. It starts with Elijah boldly telling a king named Ahab, who had rejected God, that a drought was coming. Now, no king wants to hear that there will be suffering in his land; you know people always look for someone to blame when trouble comes, and the messenger is an easy target. Still, Elijah gives Ahab the bad news, and then bravely reveals something even more infuriating: there will be neither rain nor dew for the next few years unless *Elijah* says so. So during that drought, Elijah was despised, blamed, and hunted essentially because he obeyed God.

Wouldn't all that make it easy to let fear take over? Especially when that strain dragged on for *three years*?

But Elijah didn't. For all that time, he constantly turned to God, and God constantly provided for him through miracles—ravens that brought him food, to name one of many—and even gave him power to perform miracles himself. Considering how much Elijah survived and the astonishing ways he witnessed God's presence and power, it seems like nothing could ever shake this warrior.

But the thing about fear is it just keeps reigning blows down on you. The first part of Romans 8:15 really nails fear's approach in contrast to the nature of the Holy Spirit: "The Spirit you received does not make you slaves, so that you live in fear again . . .". "That small word, "again," paints the picture of fear as a relentless and untiring enemy that desires to enslave us repeatedly. *Fear of being hated doesn't get you, Elijah? Maybe fear of starvation and thirst will. No? Let's try fear of public humiliation. You confidently batted that away?*

Let's go for a death threat.

Fight or Flight

In 1 Kings 19, the prophet-hunting queen Jezebel set her eyes on killing Elijah. Upon hearing the news, our battle-weary hero — who, after all, had just finished outrunning a king riding in his chariot while Elijah was on foot in 1 Kings 18:46—immediately bolted. Then, instead of seeking more of the miraculous provision and direction he'd seen in the past, he begged God to let him die. So after all the victories Elijah experienced, the threat of a vengeful queen took him out of battle—and Jezebel never even got to him.

Fear did.

That's bad enough; still, it's not what chills me most about Elijah's story. I'm more troubled about what he lost by letting fear take over. See, after God sent an angel to minister to and strengthen the suicidal, exhausted past champion, He directed Elijah to go back and anoint Elisha to succeed him as a prophet. In other words, as soon as fear caused Elijah to flee and fold despite his record of winning, it led to the closure of his ministry.

Ouch.

No way do I want that to happen to me.

Like Elijah, I'd seen pure miracles in my survival, so it's reasonable you might think fear would pose little threat to me anymore—that I'd be on the road to victory after victory, no sweat.

I only wish it were that easy.

I think what shocked me most about my first night back in the house was that what happened to Elijah happened to me: a simultaneous collision between fear and reaction. He bolted from the scene, and if I physically could have, I would have also. That is how powerful the tight grip of fear is; you instantly want to do whatever you can to immediately get away. Often there is no space in the moment of a threat to process it or seek counsel from the Lord or others, there is only time for a split-second choice between two options: fight or flight.

The thing is, I don't want to flee from Montana Street because of fear. I want to fight. And I want to win. So I decide, the morning after fear's first ugly attack, to wage war against it.

But how do I make sure that fear doesn't win in *my* story? How do I go the distance against this opponent aiming to hammer its way to an eventual win? Basically, by recognizing the enemy and by remembering to whom I belong—then going to Him.

Do I Belong to the Father of Lies or to Abba, Father?

Recognizing the enemy can be remarkably tricky. I'd expected an opponent to show up the first night back at the house: my attacker. The actual opponent who showed up that night, however, wasn't a person, but a spirit. It's 2 Timothy 1:7 (KJV) that explains this: "For God hath not given us the *spirit* of fear." So I began to see that the spirit of fear, which raged war *inside* of me while trying to keep me focused on an *outside* target, belonged to the father of lies who always fights dirty and tries to trick me into the wrong "solution" (running away). For me to run from 110 Montana or the inner city wouldn't defeat the spirit of fear raging war inside of me; it would just employ external situations as weapons, and those are useless in a spiritual battle.

God, on the other hand, is *extremely* useful in a spiritual battle. Fear may rage inside me, but there's another Spirit in there too, the Holy one—and it's the greater spirit, as the apostle John says in 1 John 4:3-4.

So fighting fear, I find, comes down to a question of ownership. To whom do I belong, the father of lies or Abba, Father? The Bible offers verse after verse to help me keep this straight; 1 John 4:4 specifically addresses us as "dear children" who are "from God," Romans 8:15 says in part that "the Spirit you received brought about your adoption to sonship. And by him we cry, *"Abba,* Father," and the next verse brings it home: "The Spirit himself testifies with our spirit that we are God's children" (Romans 8:16).

In other words, fighting fear includes remembering we're God's kids, lovingly handpicked and chosen to become His children. We're not alone; we have a loving Father who lives in us and fights for us, wanting nothing but the best for us. From there, it's all about going to Him. See, while the spirit of fear desires the steering wheel, so does the Spirit of Truth. He has things to say to us to help, but we have to draw close to hear them. He fights our battles, but we have to lean in to Him by renewing our mind with the Word and through prayer and worship rather than listening to and being guided by fear.

In the end, the ultimate counterpunch to fear is taking my eyes off the offender the Enemy wants me focused on, and putting them back on my Father. And this counterpunch, I discover, must be used time and time again. *That's* how you win the fight against fear; *that's* how you go the distance against an enemy that doesn't give up.

And because I know the secret to outlasting the spirit of fear centers upon my relationship as a son to my Heavenly Father, it's only fitting that I teach my son to fight with me.

Here's How I Fought Fear

The kids return home the following night, and I find the spirit of fear is once again waiting for me when it is time to go to bed, seeking to exhaust me with the thought my attacker will hurt me again. This time, I am ready to fight back the right way.

So Noah, sitting on the couch just feet away from where my attacker and I fought, reads portions of the Bible to help me remember God's presence is with us. My son starts with Psalm 46:1-5 to remind me of the truth in the face of the lies with which the Enemy is trying to wear me out.

> God is our refuge and strength, an ever-present help in trouble.
>
> Therefore we will not fear, though the earth give way and the mountains fall into the heart of the sea,
>
> though its waters roar and foam and the mountains quake with their surging.
>
> There is a river whose streams make glad the city of God, the holy place where the Most High dwells.
>
> God is within her, she will not fall; God will help her at break of day. (Psalm 46:1-5)

As Noah reads, I pace back and forth, praying in the Spirit and crying out to my Father. I worship God for my second chance. I thank Him for the people He's placed in my life, His hedge of protection over our family, and for home, the place I continually return to whenever overwhelmed emotionally or knocked down in the fight.

Noah and I keep using these spiritual weapons to fight the spirit of fear every night for weeks, until I've gained momentum in the fight against it.

At this point I've learned how to battle two things: my original perspective of being owed something, and fear. Both these opponents have worked to keep me tied to my attacker. The next battle will shift ground a little. It's not that my attacker isn't a part of it, of course. It's just that it becomes more about the fallout of what he did to me than about being upset that he did it at all, or scared he might do it again.

In other words, it's the hurts and wounds not allowed to heal cleanly or easily that cause bitterness to put on the gloves.

CHAPTER 26

ROUND 3: BITTERNESS

"I've got to go out for a little bit," Sarah says, her mind on the errands ahead of her. "Do you need something from me while I'm out and about?"

Need from you? I think. *Really.*

"I don't need *anything* from you, Sarah," I say coldly. "I'm good." Surprised by my tone, my wife pauses to look at me on her way out.

"Wow," she says. "All right then. Just let me know if something changes." The door clicks behind her.

I'm just so sick of this, I tell the Lord. Weeks have now turned into months, and I'm still dependent on other people because of the damage from the attack, especially to my hands. Five days a week, two hours a day, I spend mornings at rehab working through hand therapy. Each day I'm seeing a little more range of motion and strength in my fingers, but forcing locked joints to move is severely painful, as is awaiting progress while enduring the bad shape they're still in. Moreover, I need to be driven 30 minutes each way for the therapy; at home, I need tons of help too. I intensely dislike this; my growing bitterness about it is exactly what came out in my reaction to Sarah's innocent question.

I don't need anyone, I tell myself, heading to the kitchen. *I can take care of myself.*

I decide to prove it by trying to cook for the first time. So making one of my all-time favorite meals, Cheeseburger Hamburger Helper, becomes my weapon against feeling so vulnerable and needy. It seems to do the trick, as the sense of independence from getting everything out and cooking feels fantastic.

"See," I say softly to myself. "I don't need anyone." I'm still enjoying my newfound freedom when I settle down for a post-triumph nap.

Until a certain urgency makes itself known.

I glance toward the bathroom. I look down at my hands confined in these cursed splints. And only minutes into reveling in my independence, reality sets back in.

You almost home? I text Sarah.

She writes back quickly. *In a little bit . . . why?*

Please don't be mad at me. I poke laboriously into the phone. *I'm sorry.*

You're fine, Kev. I didn't mean anything when I asked if you needed anything. Seriously. I am glad you are good. Please don't be mad at me.

I know. I'm sorry. I'm super sorry. I mean I'm really, really sorry. I'm not usually so apologetic, but I'm realizing I need her too much to be mad at her, even as I resent depending on her. I explain that the best I can by text, in addition to telling her I cooked for myself.

But now I need to go to the bathroom. I can't because I need you tohelp. I hate these stupid splints. I hate my hands. I'm sorry.

It's okay, Kevin, Sarah texts back. *I love you.* I'm glad of that of course—but that doesn't solve a very immediate problem.

You aren't hearing me, I text back. *I need you. I have to go to the bathroom BAD but can't. You almost home? LOL*

The exchange ends up kind of funny, but the whole truth is that having a loved one have to wipe your bottom for more than two months is just humiliating.

As the span of time between the present day and the night of the attack grows longer, I find myself focusing less on the attack itself and more on the physical damage, missed opportunities, financial devastation, and the hurt my kids have suffered due to the attack—and how angry I am about all of it. At first, I just sit back and wait for these feelings to pass.

Unfortunately, that is the exact wrong move to make.

See, an opponent even more destructive and insidious than fear is now staring me down. And any fighter knows if you go limp in the ring, you're gonna get knocked out. The challenge though, is I don't see myself going limp at first. My actions seem to me a lot like fighting—just not the kind that involves God.

Instead, I'm looking for a rematch with the person responsible for this life I'm starting to hate.

In between the mentally and physically exhausting therapy for my hands, I'm spending a lot of time by myself as Sarah runs errands and carts the kids between activities in the afternoons. Fueled by a constant awareness of how Percy hurt me and mine, I begin to spend that time on a one-man manhunt, searching the Internet for clues about him. How did he get from Alabama to Michigan? Where is he now?

He's got to be caught and caught today, I'd think. So before long, Googling isn't enough.

"Is Percy there?" my shaking voice softly speaks over the cell phone.

"No, he is not. May I ask who is calling?" asks the woman on the other end of the Alabama number I just dialed. I start to stumble around explaining why I'm calling, but change my mind when I realize her Percy is not *the* Percy.

"Never mind. I'm sorry to have called you," I say, hanging up as quickly as I can. It's just one of what will be a series of seemingly close encounters that feed my growing obsession to get this guy.

Another happens when someone drops off a package addressed "To The Pastor" on the porch of a neighbor, who brings it by. Inside is some type of a voodoo-looking necklace made of a leather shoe lace with bunch of weird objects hanging from it—a claw of some bird of prey, a large shark tooth, some jagged rocks. As I take it out of the box I get an eerie and evil feeling in my gut—and that's before I open the letter enclosed.

It's an apology from an anonymous person "from the streets" for not having gone to the police when he heard my attacker bragging that he stabbed the pastor. The letter, which is unsigned, is both terrifying and electrifying. I can't wait to give it to police, then get out of town for a few days—and before returning, to buy our family's first gun.

The gun empowers me, as does the ever-increasing feeling of anger.

I hope he does come back, I begin to think. *This time, I'll be ready for him.* My obsession is starting to twist from finding the guy to hurting him, or even killing him. I push aside the fact that Sarah would actually have to shoot the gun, due to my messed-up hands. I want to feed on fuming, not facts.

With the weapon on the scene, I'm done cowering in my room; instead, I start looking out my windows hoping to catch a glimpse of him. Then, watching from inside isn't good enough; I want everyone in the neighborhood to know I'm ready for a rematch. So I take this fight to the street—literally. Nearly every day, I begin going for little walks up and down the street with my new dog Rocky, a purebred German Shepherd—very intentional little walks that fans the flames of my anger.

Over and over, I'm retracing the steps my attacker took as he left my house after the attack. Police had identified this path, going down my front steps and in the opposite direction from where I'd escaped through my side door, by the blood that dripped from my attacker as he departed.

Now, it's those spots and smears I bore my eyes into during my little strolls.

I hurt him, I say to myself. *I got the knife from him and stabbed him back when he was on top of me. I hurt him and caused him to bleed.*

Staring at anything that resembled a blood drop was invigorating; I like the pleasure I get out of the thought that I had hurt him. Now *this* is the kind of fighting that's familiar to me. I'm no longer some sad, wimpy victim willing to forgive; all thought of going to the cross and seeing myself as the offender is being rewritten in my growing obsession, and before long, the walks aren't enough either. Once I can drive, I'm jumping into the Ford Excursion my attacker couldn't find the keys to steal and driving around town looking for him.

Sarah, by the way, has no idea I'm doing this; she'd hardly be on board with me putting my still-broken body behind the wheel to feed an ugly obsession. And the truth is, it's not really the best idea, physically or mentally.

But the thing about obsession is it tends to cloud truth.

Plus the risks seem worth it when I think I spot him one day in front of the Detroit Rescue Mission Ministries office. I drag the police chief off his break and into confronting the guy as I hunker down nearby in my Excursion—only to drive off embarrassed and frustrated when it becomes obvious it's not the right guy. I realize I'd profiled a guy who was probably part of the Rescue Mission and getting his life back on track.

Way to go, pastor.

But another thing about obsession is once you feed it, it grows a life of its own. So I shake off that letdown to continue thinking *I'm going to get him* as I go back to the house. Upon returning home, I flip through the mail and find a suspicious letter addressed to me. It's from a "D Jones"—I know no one by that name—and the return address instantly startles me: Birmingham, Alabama. It makes sense I don't recognize the name, since I don't know anyone from there.

Except, of course, a guy named Percy.

Then, heart pounding, I unfold a completely blank piece of paper—and instantly, my blood boils over.

Someone is messing with me. But the police politely disagree when I turn the letter over to them.

"I don't think it's anything, Pastor," the detectives tell me. "Probably just a coincidence."

Are you *kidding* me?

"I know no one from Alabama, let alone Birmingham, and you think it's a coincidence?" I explode. "Someone is sending me a message. Someone is messing with me and I'm telling you, I'm not going to take it. You guys have got to find this guy or I will."

There's one sure-fire fuel for both anger and obsession: more of the same. So I turn back to the Internet, logging on daily to search by his name and cities he's lived in. That leads me to a Classmates.com match where I find someone by my attacker's name posting to friends. The fire in my belly burns hotter when I subscribe to the service and learn where he posted from: an address two miles from my house.

After nearly murdering me, did he use the laptop he stole from me to cheerfully greet friends before pawning it? I'm as rattled as I am riled up. I grab a weapon. I get in the car. I don't know what I'll do when I get to the address, but I have to go there.

I may not have a plan, but I have a purpose.

It will, however, be thwarted—again. The place seems to be a junk yard or a scrap yard where people might take metals to recycle for quick cash—a decent place to sell a stolen laptop, perhaps. But I can't really look into it; the building is closed off behind tall steel walls, and there's no one in sight to ask. I drive around, circling around it a few times before I give in to the mental and emotional exhaustion creeping in and head to the police station to hand over the new evidence.

Then, there's nothing to do but keep logging onto the Internet. To keep obsessing. And amidst the bitter rage increasing, to continue with rehab for my hands. I really want my hands to be more useful. Able to clench into fists—or better, to aim and fire a gun—would be ideal.

Yeah. That would be *great*.

I simply don't know, at this time, that what feels like becoming strong for a fight is going to lead me to the most beaten place of my life.

CHAPTER 27

RIPPING UP ROOTS

The ultimate low point happens one day when I am driving home after an exhausting day of rehab following a restless night of sleep consumed with thoughts of finding this guy. It comes in the form of an idea just popping into my head.

Kill yourself.

End your life.

Drive into the concrete overpass and just end this misery.

As quickly as these thoughts come to mind, they depart—but I still lose it, weeping in the face of thinking about taking my life.

"What's wrong with me?" I shout out loud between sobs. After all that had happened—my life being spared, my family together, physically healing and becoming stronger each day, surrounded by friends and family who love me—why in the world would I contemplate, even for a second, ending my life? What's behind this fleeting thought?

As it so often does, the Bible helped unlock the mystery. It starts with me examining Hebrews 12:15, which warns against letting a "bitter root" grow to cause trouble, referring to Esau, who in the Old Testament had been wronged by his brother Jacob. I quickly saw that being hurt led to Esau becoming a person associated not only having a root of bitterness but to something far beyond anger or revenge: immorality. I realized I too had developed a bitter root that resulted in bad fruit—in my case, suicidal thoughts. Then one day, I heard a sermon by Pastor Tim that helped me see how extremely dangerous bitterness, and the thoughts that come from it, can be.

See, Ahithophel, the seemingly minor Old Testament character that Pastor Tim preached on, didn't just have suicidal thoughts, he ended up actually strangling himself.

The High Costs of Bitterness

Ahithophel, whose story begins in 2 Samuel 15:12, was a highly acclaimed adviser to David; Scripture goes so far as to say "every word Ahithophel spoke seemed as wise as though it had come directly from the mouth of God" (2 Samuel 16:23, NLT). Yet, by the end of the chapter, David is told Ahithophel is among the conspirators with Absalom, David's own son who had turned against him.

In other words, Ahithophel went from Team David to Team Absalom in a major coup in the battle to dethrone David and elevate Absalom to the position of king.

But there's more. Ahithophel didn't just switch loyalty, he developed a new mission: to hunt and destroy David. (For obvious reasons, that gets my attention.) Why? When you study Ahithophel's family line carefully, you realize there had to have been a bitter root that most likely grew from a hurt buried in his heart. David hurt him by derailing the life of Bathsheba, the married woman David slept with in one of the most-told Bible stories of all time. Bathsheba, of course, became pregnant and David, attempting to cover up his sin, murdered her husband Uriah. Then, the child born as a result of this sin died. All of which had to be extremely painful for Ahithophel.

See, Bathsheba was Ahithophel's granddaughter.

Any grandparent knows there is a particular kind of love one has toward their grandkids. Children can do wrong—grandkids, never! That's the position Ahithophel was in as he watched Bathsheba mourn the loss of her husband, then her child, only to discover the man with whom he was sharing his wise counsel—and for whom his own son Eliam, Bathsheba's father, risked his life as one of David's mighty men—was responsible. It isn't much of a leap to imagine what Ahithophel must have battled in the face of what surely was a huge amount of pain, hurt, betrayal, and anger. Suddenly, Ahithophel's suicide doesn't seem quite so crazy—or hard to relate to, either. I can imagine Ahithophel's thoughts of revenge for David were as obsessive as mine while I spent weeks pursuing a man named Percy, and it seems obvious they led to the same dark thoughts.

Pastor Tim's message about Ahithophel helped me realize suicidal thoughts are about the heart, more than the mind. Feelings and emotions that grow out of being hurt support unhealthy attitudes and behaviors—like anger, spite, jealousy, hatred, slander, gossip, and revenge—that if not fought, inevitably lead to fruits like addictions, unkind or abusive behavior, depression, and even suicide. They don't go away if ignored (like when I tried to just sit back and wait for the feelings to pass), they get worse.

Looking back, it makes so much sense. But I honestly didn't see it all the time I was Googling and plotting; I was too distracted by what felt like a newfound sense of power, something that appealed to me going way back to my Rambo nickname. That's another way the Enemy can go after any fighter who has taken a beating: *look at what happened to you.* In my case, *look how your physical, emotional, and mental wellbeing, your ability to connect with others, your work, your finances, your sense of home, your parenting are decimated. Try to get revenge, or if you can't, at least escape. Not up for literal suicide? There are a million ways to throw in the towel. Stop trying to connect with others. Become a distracted employee. Ignore financial commitments and responsibilities. Give up trying to parent your kids.*

Only, that's not what I want. What I want . . . what I want . . . oh right; it's starting to come back to me. I'd been wanting to discover the exciting possibilities locked in God's plans to use what was intended for evil for good.

I'm reminded that Jesus, right after hearing "This is my Son, whom I love; with him I am well pleased" in Matthew 3:17, was tempted by the devil to end His life by throwing himself down from the pinnacle of the temple in Matthew 4:5. Thank God the Enemy lost in his efforts to assassinate God's yet-unfulfilled plans in Jesus' life; I want him to lose in my life too. Clearly, I needed to re-up the *right* kind of fighting.

I'm so glad God speaks to the deepest areas of my life—especially when they provide much-needed warnings. See, like I don't want Elijah's loss-of-ministry finale when battling fear, I don't want Ahithophel's loss-of-life finale when battling anger and bitterness. I don't even want to end up like Esau; he may not have committed suicide, but he sure did get bitter and never better. People still need me, and I want to be able to offer them the good fruit that come from a life that has ripped out roots of bitterness and planted a seed of forgiving just as Christ forgave me.

So bitterness, it's time to stop lurking around; step on out into the spotlight, where we can have a fair fight.

How to Fight Bitterness

If I'm going to deal with the unhealthy attitudes and behaviors that are becoming visible, then I must begin ripping up roots. For that, I learn the key is faith: praying for increased faith, and figuring out what specific faith words a person needs to speak to get free from bitterness.

Part of the reason the fight to forgive gets really challenging when you start to go rounds against bitterness is this opponent tends to stay out of sight so long that the roots grow strong and deep before they're exposed. So battling them requires a heavy hitter. Fortunately, we have help in our corner, and the disciples showed us how to call on Him in Luke 17:5: "The apostles said to the Lord, 'Increase our faith!'" We can pray the same exact thing, any time. And check out how Jesus answered that prayer—by literally connecting faith with ripping up roots—in the very next verse: "If you have faith as small as a mustard seed, you can say to this mulberry tree, 'Be uprooted and planted in the sea,' and it will obey you" (Luke 17:6). So, it's clear faith is a must.

But faith, in and of itself, isn't enough to rip up roots of bitterness; there's another key right there in Luke 17:6. Remember, Jesus said that if you have faith you can *say*, "Be uprooted and planted in the sea," and the mulberry tree will obey you. In other words, having faith just empowers you; it's what you *say* that causes change.

So I need to speak faith; got it. But *what* should I say now that things are so bad that suicidal thoughts are trying to get my attention? Do I get all spiritual and begin speaking in old King James Bible language with my best preacher voice, "be uprooteth ye spirit of hatred and ye evil desires to hurteth the one who hath hurteth me"?

I don't think so. See, love has a different language, I discover in another lesson from Jesus:

But I say unto you which hear, Love your enemies, do good to them which hate you. Bless them that curse you, and pray for them which despitefully use you. (Luke 6:27-28, KJV)

In other words, you don't address or battle your feelings directly; you fight by praying for the very person you're so angry with, in opposition to bitterness and in harmony with God's Word. It's the sucker punch the Enemy just doesn't expect from a fighter who has been battling bitterness.

In fact, employing this powerful language is what eventually puts bitterness down for the count.

Here's How I Fought Bitterness

After a good cry following the rogue thoughts of suicide, I started doing the second part of Luke 6:27-28: blessing and interceding for Percy.

God, bless Percy today in some way, I prayed. He needs You. Keep him safe, God, and do a work in His life. Put people in his path who will minister to his hurts and pains. Forgive him today for what he did to me. Forgive him for any hurt he has caused others. Pursue Percy, Lord and capture his heart, mind, and spirit. May he come to know you in a real and intimate way today. I bless him today in the name of Jesus. Amen.

It's pretty hard to continue wanting to enact some type of revenge on someone when you begin praying over his life daily. Right feelings don't bring about right choices, but right choices—in this case, putting God's word into action—will eventually produce right feelings.

So my glove wasn't raised in the air that first day I fought bitterness; actually, it took many, many months of daily pronouncing blessings over the life of my attacker to truly see an impact. At first, I'll admit, I did it only because I didn't like what I was becoming. Over time, however, I was amazed at the healing I experienced when I no longer desired revenge.

Now, if only I could flashbacks of that night. do something about the reoccurring

If only I could forget.

CHAPTER 28
ROUND 4: FLASHBACKS

Sirens with their red-and-blue lights flashing in the dark instantly remind me of being on my neighbor's porch the night of the attack.

Quick, sudden turns of my head create the same electrical twinges that shot through my body the night of the attack, and my memory flashes back to my attacker stabbing me.

Whenever I use the big knife in my knife block, I can't keep my mind from going to *the* knife that caused the scars that remind me daily of what happened; I find myself picturing how I got this one or that one, over and over. Sometimes, I'll find myself stabbing at a steak to try to picture how deep the knife went into my body, sort of experimenting with what it took to create certain scars.

At times, I find myself out of control not just of my memories but of my reactions. Even the slightest sounds in or around the house at night—the kids getting in or out of bed, the dog jumping on furniture or walking up the stairs—send me into a full adrenaline rush; if I hear a dog bark at night, I instantly grab a gun. Seeing or touching a tennis racket causes a quick mental cataloging of other options I now keep on hand, such as my gun and bat.

I don't have the kind of flashbacks often associated with war veterans, where their present reality is shaken to the point where they perceive they're back in combat. Still, while I don't literally think I'm there again when sights, sounds, feelings, and thoughts flash my mind back to the night of the attack, these memories do cause me to become stuck replaying what is behind me.

Flashbacks can be very, very distracting.

Even though such moments are brief, the emotional recalibration needed to force myself back to the present is exhausting, as is coping with the lingering impact of flashbacks. It's hard to be as kind or as patient as you want to be when you've already used up your energy trying to bounce back from being hijacked by memories, and the guilt of having less to give to others is heavy.

So I desperately want to shut down these memories, and I find I'm back to obsessing about justice, the way I was before I returned to the cross, in hopes it will get me free—until one day in November 2009 when the state's prosecutor in Alabama presents me with a startling good news/bad news scenario.

Good news: Percy is off the streets. After three months on the run, he has been arrested 760 miles away in Birmingham, Alabama for committing another crime.

Bad news: I'm told if convicted for his other crime, Percy would have to serve out that sentence—which is estimated to be 10 to 20 years—before being extradited to Michigan to face justice for the crimes committed against me.

In other words, the justice I'm desperately counting on to help me move on is within reach but can't be pursued right away. With that news, I can almost feel shackles being placed around my ankles, keeping me bound to what's "supposed to" be behind me.

That's what everyone seems to think—that the attack is a part of the past, not the present. And I kind of get it, especially when a couple more months pass. Concluding five months of physical therapy ushered in a new year, and 2010 sees my days freed from those constant appointments. Now that I'm as good as I'm going to get physically, I'm driving my kids to school every day and attending Noah's middle school soccer games. Our family is attending church together weekly. To onlookers, my life appears to be back to normal for me.

But it isn't back to normal; it never will be, if normal is defined as the way things used to be. Furthermore, I'm surprised to find I don't actually *want* life to go back to the way it was before the attack. I'm not sure if this is good or bad. Could it be a sign of the deeper damage that some seem to think will arise in me? Or is this pointing to the greater purpose that could come out of it all? In any case, is there a way to get unstuck?

As with any deeply troubling questions, these are good ones to take right to God in prayer. So I do, regularly getting up early to go to the church and pray by myself before anyone else comes in.

Lord, something has to change, I pray. It's time! I can't remain stuck for twenty years until I hear my attacker's response to the wrongs he is responsible for, so what do I do? My scars distract me. My memories control me. If I stay put much longer, chained to the past, I feel as if a part of me is going to die.

Help me Lord. How do I move forward with these uninvited scars and the memories of what produced them?

It isn't long before God begins to show me that though these powerful memories and flashbacks can work against me, they also can work for me—and for future good. It starts when I read a piece by Pastor John

Ortberg titled "Don't Waste a Crisis."[vii] In it, he perfectly described the inner battle I was facing concerning my past, and I knew I needed to reach out to him despite never having met him before. When we speak in February 2010, Pastor Ortberg begins by talking about how normal life is like being on a treadmill.

"We're just running after our duties, our normal schedule, money, success, education, comfort, security, pleasure, happiness— sometimes we don't even know what, we're just running after it," he says. "And then when suffering comes, it just knocks you off the treadmill, and all of a sudden you have to ask, 'What in the world am I doing here? Is there any meaning to this life?'"

That is exactly what I am feeling and facing.

Pastor Ortberg continues, "A lot of times, people go through suffering and they see things differently, and they say to themselves, 'You know what? I'm going to keep this new perspective the rest of my life.'" But usually they don't, he says. "Sooner or later normal life sucks you back into its vortex, and when it does, you lose all the benefit you could have gotten out of suffering if you had actually taken action when it happened."

Next, Pastor Ortberg introduces me to the gift of change available when suffering comes; I can grab onto it if I want to, he explains.

"Kevin," he says, "if you have the courage to make actual changes now to your lifestyle, friendships, priorities, pursuits, habits, goals, schedule— essentially, to where you spend your time and energy— your suffering will turn into the greatest gift you'd never have experienced otherwise."

[vii] John Ortberg, "Don't Waste a Crisis: Crises, While Unwanted, Are Windows of Opportunity for the Cure of Souls," *Christianity Today* 32, No. 1 (Winter 2011)

Wow. Harnessing the power of flashbacks and using it to keep me off the treadmill—thus making room for God to lead me in a new direction and do something amazing through my shifted perspective—sure sounds a lot more exciting than being stuck in the memories. So as Pastor Ortberg kindly prays for me, I start realizing God doesn't want flashbacks to *become* my path, but to create a *new* path.

Which brings me back to Joseph, our Christlike hero of Genesis 50:20. If the formula for the gift of change Pastor Ortberg talked about is an interruption of the norm, suffering, and then transformation, Joseph certainly experienced it:

- He was knocked off the treadmill of ordinary life when he was betrayed and thrown into a pit by his brothers, then sold into slavery.

- He certainly suffered by losing years with his dad, being falsely accused of a sexual assault, going to prison for a crime he didn't commit, and getting forgotten by those who made promises to help.

- And that he was changed is undeniable. The self-absorbed teenager consumed with his own dreams in Genesis 37 was not only unrecognizable in appearance, but also in character in Genesis 45 as a thirty-nine-year-old adult helping the brothers who had betrayed him 22 years earlier.

But how did Joseph get there? Surely he battled his own flashbacks. A tug on his clothing bringing him back to his brothers stripping him of his robe, maybe. Perhaps thudding sounds jerked his mind back to what it felt like for his body to slam against the bottom of the pit. Clanging or musty smells could have consistently reminded him of being locked up in prison. I can't imagine he came out of what he'd been through without any scars. Regardless, his life demonstrated he'd experienced the gift of change, and I wanted to see what happened.

So I began examining his life, and I discovered something incredible about five years before he was reunited with his estranged brothers, approximately seventeen or eighteen years after he was wronged by his family of origin.

God empowered Joseph to forget.

It's right there in Genesis 41:51, which tells us Joseph named his firstborn Manasseh—a name commonly associated with "forget"—and said, "It is because God has made me forget all my trouble and all my father's household." If God could make Joseph forget after all the crazy stuff that happened to him, then surely there's hope for me! It's a thrilling thought for someone haunted each and every day by memories.

Discovering this overlooked testimony is exactly what I need to put Pastor Ortberg's encouragement into action. I become determined not to get back on the treadmill; I am going to make room for God to make me forget and change me.

God, make me forget Percy, I begin praying daily. *I'm tired of always thinking about what he is doing, what he has done, what he is thinking, and if he will ever own up to his actions. God, make me forget the hurt, pain, and the memories I return to when I see the scars upon my body; I want to move forward and I need to forget it all.*

Make me forgive and forget all my troubles like You did for Joseph.

It's a good thing Joseph's words about God making him forget struck such a strong chord in me; it would take some serious commitment to find my footing. For the longest time it seemed like the more I prayed and asked for God to make me forget, the more—and more intensely—I found myself recalling what had happened.

In time, though, I came to recognize Biblical forgetting is different from losing the ability or tendency to recall what happened. When God promises in passages including Hebrews 8:12, Hebrews 10:17, and Isaiah 43:25 to remember our sins no more, He is not suggesting that He will have a bad memory! That would be impossible with God; He is all-knowing. What God *is* saying is, "I will no longer hold their sins against them. I will not allow their sins to affect their relationship with Me or influence My attitude toward them."

Thank God! What a relief to realize Biblical forgetting does not suggest an impossible feat of mental and psychological gymnastics by which we try to erase our history. Instead, I see Biblical forgetting as finding a way to see the past become powerless—at least in any negative way—in my today. It's encouraging to think that while I may not be able to control my memories, I can control what impact those memories have on my choices; I may not be able to change my past, but I can stop allowing my past to own me.

That leaves just one all-important question: *how* do you forget the Biblical way?

CHAPTER 29

RUNNING FROM THE LEAD

Have you ever found your attention suddenly drawn to someone who is hurting?

It can be the woman checking your groceries at the store—you notice a heaviness to her reluctant words as she mechanically moves the items over the belt. Or a guy who is usually the center of any gathering that you see standing quietly off to the side instead. Or the family member you realize is preoccupied and emotionally unavailable during what should be a happy occasion.

For Joseph, it was his fellow prisoners. Genesis 40:6 tells us Joseph saw that two of these men were dejected.

"Why do you look so sad today?" he asked them kindly in the next verse.

Now, Joseph had plenty of his own troubles, what with being stuck in prison essentially for doing right (resisting the advances of his boss's wife, who paid him back by accusing him of attempted rape). He had to have wondered how he could explain his innocence to someone, anyone, perhaps doubting people would listen to a man locked up like a common criminal. There's no way of knowing, really; Scripture doesn't tell us much about Joseph's thoughts in Genesis 39 and 40.

It just talks about his actions.

During Joseph's prison time—long before the Lord empowered him to forget all his troubles—he spent years both serving people in charge and fellow prisoners. Serving Potiphar and the warden is one thing; he *had* to serve them. But he was under no obligation to serve his fellow prisoners, and I notice his transformation really began when he started noticing *their* hurts, taking the time to inquire what was wrong, and serving them with his giftings, including the interpretation of dreams.

Could it be that serving others—specifically, prisoners—was key to Joseph forgetting over the years? I wonder, and something begins to click in me; what if I were to look for ways to serve men who have spent a lot of time in prison, like my attacker?

So I begin talking with people who have spent time in prison and reading up on the shockingly high rate at which men fall back into the prison system after being released, as Percy had. The National Institute of Justice website quotes one study[viii] that found within five years of release, about three-quarters (76.6 percent) of released prisoners were rearrested, more than half (56.7 percent) of those by the end of the first year out of prison. One of the greatest factors, I learn, is the hard time they have getting employment with a felony on their record.

This catches my attention—after all, one of the joys of the inflatables business I ran and sold just before the attack was employing and training people who badly needed jobs. The next thing I know, Pastor Tim and I are sitting on my couch while I tell him how I want to

---

[viii] Matthew R. Durose, Alexia D. Cooper, and Howard N. Snyder, "Recidivism of Prisoners Released in 30 States in 2005: Patterns from 2005 to 2010." *Bureau of Justice Statistics Special Report* (April 2014)

create a business where I can employ and help former prisoners. It had to be a bit of a shock for Pastor Tim; I'm sure me returning to the business world sounded like a step backward, not forward, since I had just transitioned away from my inflatables business right before the attack to focus solely on ministry. Still, he encouraged me, telling me to take the following couple months to begin praying and working that through.

"I'm behind you," he says. So I develop a donation program for churches to hold a campaign to obtain items while working on developing the systems around a process of selling them that would allow me to employ former prisoners, starting with an ex- gang leader with whom I meet.

Serving others can be very, very liberating.

Remember, Biblical forgetting is about getting free from the negative power of the past. In time, God would teach me that putting that into practice is all about three things: position, pace, and pursuit.

Sound like a race to you? It did to Paul too.

How to Forget the Biblical Way

I found my fight strategy for *how* to forget through the apostle Paul's great race analogy in Philippians 3:13-14. Sounding like a powerful athlete who had completely forgotten the opponents coming up behind him in a race he was still running, Paul wrote: "Brothers and sisters, I do not consider myself yet to have taken hold of it. But one thing I do: Forgetting what is behind and straining toward what is ahead, I press on toward the goal to win the prize for which God has called me heavenward in Christ Jesus."

With that, Paul gave us an awesome fighting strategy for becoming oblivious to what is trying to overtake us. I see it in three essential parts:

1. **"Forgetting what is behind"** refers to choosing a *position* that puts our opponent—the past—behind us. I call this "running from the lead" because it is choosing to lead memories instead of being led by them; forgetting only becomes possible when you're running from the lead.

2. **"Straining toward what is ahead"** speaks to our *pace;* there's a necessary speed at which we have to run to maintain the lead. Sometimes I think of this as "the lean." Every runner who is fighting to win will be leaning forward with arms pumping and legs running hard, and a person can't both lean toward what's ahead and put their eyes on what's behind them as well; glancing over the shoulder would require slowing down and straightening up. We have to pick whether to lean forward or look back, and the only way to lean or strain forward is to be running at a really fast pace.

3. **"Press on toward the goal"** refers to our *pursuit* of a new target. It has to do with the "what" we are reaching toward, something that is "ahead"—having to do with the future, not the past—that provides a focus to replace obsessing on anything in the past that threatens to hijack us emotionally, spiritually, mentally, or physically.

Really, Paul pulled it all together for me. I see that overtaking the lead from the person who wronged me, running with purpose toward my future, and passionately pursuing a new, specific goal are the keys to Biblical forgetting and my ticket out of being controlled by memories I can't erase. That sounds good to me! I've spent enough time looking backward, and I'm realizing every check of the Department of Corrections website or moment focusing on my memories and what came of them is a wasted patch of time I could be actively pursuing something new, something exciting, something that can take my focus off the past and put it onto God's intended good.

Here's How I Ran from the Lead

So I find my worthy goal—serving ex-offenders and struggling men in our community—and whenever memories fight to take the lead again, I focus on "the lean," picking up the pace each month in developing what I think could be an incredible opportunity to change lives. By doing so, I am leading how this battle goes; my memories are pushed out of place by serving others.

Nine months after the attack, and after two months of working exclusively on this new vision God has given me, I decide to try to balance my new mission with serving Revival Tabernacle by returning to a pastoral role there under Pastor Tim. It doesn't take long, however, to realize I have to fully embrace change or return to the way life was before; I really can't do both. So with a heavy heart, I submit my letter of resignation in June 2010. December 31 is set to be my last day as a pastor at Revival Tabernacle; after that, I plan to focus full-time on developing a non-profit organization called Hope Village Detroit.

Resigning from Revival Tabernacle is one of the toughest decisions I've ever made; it also gives me a new lease on life. While transitioning between ministry responsibilities, I am managing successful donation campaigns with churches in Michigan, Illinois, and Indiana. I am running from the lead, and I am running fast and hard.

Then, I hit a wall.

With my final day just two months away, I face Pastor Tim on my couch again, this time with his wife Cindy. Once again, a stunning revelation hangs in the air between us—only this time, it is my turn to be stunned.

The Dilenas are leaving the church to take a position with Brooklyn Tabernacle; it's to be announced in two weeks.

But I resigned first and am done December 31, I instantly think. Outwardly I voice encouragement and excitement for Pastor Tim, but it is incredibly unsettling. Although we've technically resigned, I know how devastating having the founding pastor leave is, especially when he's as beloved as Pastor Tim, so I feel pressure to help ease the transition. Before long, the uncertainty about the future of the church distracts me from running from the lead with my ministry for men and former prisoners, and the old memories and obsessiveness about Percy threaten to overtake me again. This comes to a head one day when I cry out to God while driving to pick up my kids from school.

"What am I supposed to do now?" I shout from the top of my lungs in my car. God doesn't condemn my outburst, nor me questioning him. He just answers with words as clear as "they still need you" the night of the attack.

"This church was there for you when you needed them most," I hear. *"Make yourself available to them. Serve in any way they need you, for this is going to be the most difficult time of their lives."*

I'm so thankful for a relationship with the Holy Spirit who can speak to the deepest parts of our lives at any given moment. I'm quickly shown I'm not done running from the lead, I just need to focus my pursuit toward the church members I love deeply, and for whom I am so thankful. In other words, I still have in hand what I need to deal with my flashbacks; I can always put my eyes straightforward, I can always focus on helping others. Besides, there are hurting people everywhere.

I'm amazed at how God works and leads our lives through seasons. I'd always said the one position I'd never take was the one following the greatest preacher in America, Pastor Tim. Now here I am, doing the very thing I said I'd never do. And while I'm nowhere near the pastor nor preacher Pastor Tim is, God is still able to use me to help me serve the church during a very difficult and emotional transition. So months pass by quickly with little further awareness on my part of the silence about Percy's path to justice; I am too busy running from the lead to allow the case to affect me.

Mostly, anyway. Like anything in the sticky, tricky fight to forgive, relief is neither instant nor complete. There are still moments when the memories get the upper hand. I learn, though, I can deal with that, as long as they don't win in the end.

God really is a master of timing. In March 2011 a year into lead pastoring, and just about the time I really get that running from the lead is critical to overcoming my traumatic memories—the phone rings.

"Kevin, this is Mary, the district attorney from Birmingham, Alabama. I wanted to be the first to contact you and let you know that your prayers have been answered.

"It is going to happen in May."

CHAPTER 30

ROUND 5: CLOSURE

With one phone call, the twenty-year wait I'd finally accepted becomes a two-month wait for Percy's extradition from Alabama to Michigan for an arraignment hearing at the Highland Park court building.

It will be the first time I will see him since the night I stared straight into his eyes as he stabbed me over and over again.

I don't know much about the hearing, just that I will have to share what happened as part of the process whereby the court decides if there is enough evidence to press charges and if so, what bond to set. So there's nothing for me to do until then but keep running from the lead by serving people while I wait for some sort of closure.

Sometimes, the serving goes both ways, like with one soft-spoken young woman named Rojena who comes to the church one day and ends up blessing me at least as much as I do her.

Rojena had stopped by to ask if I would be willing to pray for her. I can't remember the last time—or if ever—someone came to the church only wanting prayer; most requests are about food or money.

"I'm sorry to bother you, pastor," says Rojena, a frail, very skinny woman with a young child in a stroller. "I came to church here about a month ago, and the service really encouraged me. I'm sorry I haven't been back, it's just hard to come when I don't even know if I want to live any more." She has a boyfriend, but he sounds like more of a taker than a giver, and she isn't sure she even wants to be with him anymore. I can tell it is not a healthy relationship for her, that her timidity is a result of his harshness. Rojena is obviously hurting deeply, and for about twenty minutes, I hurt with her, listening to her cry and share.

"I love my kids, and I feel like such a failure. They deserve so much better," Rojena says brokenly. "Will you just pray for me, pastor? I don't need anything. I just need God to help me be a better mom for my kids and to make the right decisions."

Listening to Rojena, it strikes me that we really have a lot in common. We both are facing uncertainties, but longing for change in our lives and situations. As much as Rojena thinks she needs me to pray for her, I need her to pray for me. It is a joy to pray together, identify some needs she has that the church can help meet, and offer her some hope and encouragement. It's amazing how much encouragement I get myself from serving and being served by this struggling young mom. I never will see her at church again, though I'll think of and pray for her often in the following months while I wait for the arraignment.

Then, the wait that once seemed like it would never end comes to an abrupt halt with a startling call on May 24, 2011.

"Kevin?" It's the lead detective in my investigation on the other end of the phone. "The arraignment has been moved up two hours; you have maybe a half hour to get to the courtroom."

Panic sets in. Sarah can't get there in twenty to thirty minutes; I'll have to go alone. And to top it off, the nearly two years since the attack melt away as the thoughts and feelings from that night return with hurricane force. As I scramble to get to the courtroom, there is simply no time to use a time-consuming tool like running from the lead to combat the flashbacks that begin rapidly firing in my mind; I have no choice but to trust a God with an infinite ability to get me through it.

"God, help me to not be overtaken or led down a dark path when I see him." I whisper softly as police officers escort me into the courthouse to help me avoid the media. *"Give me courage to speak your words and continue moving forward. I can't look or go backwards. I've come too far."* Still, I am incredibly anxious. Prayer or no prayer, all my thoughts are on August 4, 2009, Percy, what I've faced and what's about to happen in the packed courtroom.

Until the door to the waiting room for those testifying opens to the sound of sobbing. One of the two women in the room is borderline hysterical, burying her head in her heads wailing "I can't do it!" as the district attorney tries to comfort her and assure her she is safe. Before long, she's gently removed from the room.

"Is she going to be okay?" I ask the two officers in the room. "Is there anything I can do?" I almost feel stupid asking to help a lady who is obviously overwhelmed by intense fear when I am just as frightened about coming face-to-face with my attacker. But God makes that seem unimportant in the moment.

One officer explains, "I don't think so. She was so badly beaten by her boyfriend—it was one of the worst I've ever seen—and she doesn't want to press charges because she is scared of what will happen if he is freed."

Oh man. My heart breaks for this terrified woman. I'm still hoping I can help when she is brought back in a few minutes later and seated across from me at the large conference table. When I glance up at her, chills run up and down my body. I know this woman.

It's Rojena.

It's been two months since I'd prayed for and with her at the church, two months of wondering what happened to her from there. My heart sinks as I register what she's been through.

"Rojena?" I say gently. "It's me. Pastor Kevin." As I speak, she lifts her head and loses it at the sight of a familiar face.

"Pastor Kevin," she erupts, sobbing, "I can't do this! He beat me and I am so afraid. I can't go out there and face him. I can't do this."

In an instant, Percy, what happened to me, my suffering, and my fears just flat-out disappear, and I see the sudden change of the arraignment hearing timing as an orchestration of the Lord—a blessing, not a curse. I've been given someone to focus on in place of obsessing on my own fears and memories, and Rojena has been given a comforting, friendly face to minister to her in what might be the worst moment of her life.

God isn't done yet. As I begin ministering to Rojena, speaking scriptures of God's love and being a safe refuge for her, the woman next to her who'd been quiet up to this point begins crying; she also is an abuse victim. So during the next twenty minutes, waiting to be called to testify in my case, I find myself running from the lead again by serving two fellow prisoners to fear. By the time my name is called to head to the courtroom, I'm not even thinking about what I am about to face, only about the two ladies and their renewed courage.

It is amazing what God did in that room in all of our lives.

Following that meeting orchestrated by God, the moment I'd been obsessing about on and off since the attack is remarkably anticlimactic.

Percy and I have no dramatic reintroduction; he doesn't even make eye contact with me, sitting quietly by his defense attorney's side. In fact, she rattles me more than he does when she tries to discredit my ability to identify Percy during questioning; that gets under my skin a little, considering I've spent nearly two years working to shake off images of him from that horrible night. However, it is only fifteen or twenty minutes of answering argumentative questions from her (and clear ones from the state's prosecutor) before the judge decides to hold Percy for trial, setting bond at $450,000.

A few minutes later, I find myself alone in the same room where I'd been praying with the two victims of domestic violence just a half hour before—and I quickly find God has one more breakthrough moment for me in there.

I feel my heart overtaken with compassion and pain for Percy for the first time.

Tears flood my eyes, breathing becomes complicated by the huge knot in my throat, and I begin weeping, knowing that Percy's life will be forever changed for the worse by me telling the truth about what he did. I get to leave this courtroom a free person; he left handcuffed to be a prisoner for many, many years, if not the rest of his life. I can't imagine what he is feeling.

It isn't long before I am ushered out of the room again. As police officers escorted me through the courthouse a different way to once again avoid the media, I realized that while I hurt for Percy, I'm also experiencing pure relief at the thought my attacker won't be returned to the streets. Now I should be able to relax about being surprised by him suddenly showing up in front of me.

Except, it turns out, in this very moment.

Somehow, suddenly, Percy is standing within two feet of me, being taken back to jail as I'm being escorted out of the building. He is handcuffed, but he is *right there*, and my mind starts racing. What should I do? Retaliate? Run away? Hide behind an officer? Avoid him? As the officers throw verbal jabs at him about the high bond price, I end up just staring at Percy with a stone cold look hoping he will see me and that I'm not afraid of him anymore. He doesn't look, though.

The rest of the journey getting to my car is a blur; at first I am mostly recovering from bumping into Percy. But as I drive home to my family, I start to think about what had happened right before that—when, in one beautiful moment, compassion rose up.

Then it dawns on me that God really is helping me win this fight to forgive.

Living with the right perspective, and having knocked out fear, bitterness, and being a prisoner to my past, I'm continuing to move forward. I have ten months ahead of me before dealing with the case to spend serving my church and the hurting people God will bring across my path.

Confrontation didn't really bring the closure I've been wanting, but then, it isn't over yet. Still to come is the day in court when the person who has been subject to a crime traditionally gives a victim's statement.

For that I face one simple choice: to focus on how I've been wronged, or allow God to change the end of my story the way He did Joseph's.

CHAPTER 31

REFRAMING THE STORY

Joseph could have starved his brothers for the hardship they caused him. Literally. He had power over the food in his land during a time of extreme famine.

Sell ME into slavery, will you, he could have thought with satisfaction, using his powerful position to watch his brothers pay for their jealous choices as young men. *See how you like being forced to suffer.*

Or at least he could have really slammed them. Sometime in the twenty-two years since his brothers hurt him, Joseph had to have thought about what he might say if given a once-in-a-lifetime opportunity to unload on them with no consequences. But when he finally had the chance, what he did instead made him my ultimate coach for the final round in the fight to forgive.

The truth is, I need a great coach; detailing my suffering when finally given an opportunity to personally address Percy is definitely the obvious path. In fact, Sarah and I have been instructed to tell the court every single thing that took place that night and since, from thoughts of suicide to having to file bankruptcy to moving three times in less than two years.

"You are the victim," the district attorney told us. "Let everyone know exactly what that looks like."

I can't shake the feeling, though, that God has other ideas, especially when I start spending time in Genesis 45:1-15 and see how Joseph chose a very different path when, years after serving, leading, and being a father, he got to speak directly to the ones responsible for so much pain:

- He cried his heart out; the Bible says "he wept so loudly that the Egyptians heard him, and Pharaoh's household heard about it." Let me tell you, to know that even a champion and hero like Joseph could get overwhelmed emotionally when revisiting people and wrongs after twenty-two long years is comforting; it seems like an assurance that it is okay for me to still be emotional after two years.

- Then he revealed himself, and when his brothers became afraid, he did something a little crazy: he told the brothers who threw him in a pit the last time he was near them to "come close to me." Whoa! I think back on that weird hallway encounter with Percy right after the arraignment; the last thing I had expected or wanted was to be up close to him. Not having seen it coming, I'd had no idea how to handle it then; now, I'm wondering if "come close to me" is telling me something about how I should handle future contact with Percy. A scary but intriguing thought.

- Then Joseph just acknowledged the facts: "I am your brother Joseph, the one you sold into Egypt!" He had every right to let his brothers have it, in my opinion, and he kept it simple. I think back to the police officers jeering at Percy about the high bond price issued; as much as I wanted to prove I wasn't afraid when Percy was suddenly right before me, I also felt really uncomfortable about the police officers rubbing his nose in his guilt that way. And here I'm seeing Joseph go a totally different way.

- Finally, Joseph introduced a new character—God—to the story, then proved the Lord had made him forget by celebrating the forgiveness, good, blessings, new perspectives, life change, and opportunities that otherwise would not have taken place:

"And now, do not be distressed and do not be angry with yourselves for selling me here, because it was to save lives that God sent me ahead of you. For two years now there has been famine in the land, and for the next five years there will be no plowing and reaping. But God sent me ahead of you to preserve for you a remnant on earth and to save your lives by a great deliverance.

"So then, it was not you who sent me here, but God. He made me father to Pharaoh, lord of his entire household and ruler of all Egypt. Now hurry back to my father and say to him, 'This is what your son Joseph says: God has made me lord of all Egypt. Come down to me; don't delay. You shall live in the region of Goshen and be near me—you, your children and grandchildren, your flocks and herds, and all you have. I will provide for you there, because five years of famine are still to come. Otherwise you and your household and all who belong to you will become destitute.'" (Genesis 45:5-11)

Wow. *That's* what a "victim's statement" looked like to Joseph.

Wow.

Let it go, Joseph was saying, and clearly he had, completely reframing his story by simply proceeding in a hero's manner: as a victor, not a victim, all thanks to God. Wounds had become scars, and those scars began to serve a purpose in his life rather than leading or running it. Joseph was all about two things in this passage. First, he focused on bringing God into the center of his story in absolute celebration of what the Lord had done. Second, he focused on what he has to offer his brothers, wanting to help and establish a relationship with them, and he went on to live that out throughout Genesis. In fact, Genesis 50:20—the verse I love about how God intended what happened for the saving of many lives—wasn't the end of the story; Joseph went on to provide for, speak kindly to, and live among his one-time offenders for a total of seventy-one years after reframing his story with God in the center.

Reading Genesis 45:1-15 feels like God putting Joseph in my corner, spraying water in my mouth, wiping my brow, and pumping me up with encouragement. As the sentencing draws near, I find myself hunting through Joseph's triumph for tips on what to do when given my chance to confront my wrongdoer and wondering if I will ever get to a place of completely forgiving just as Joseph forgave his brothers, and how Christ completely forgives me. I mean Jesus, despite all of my sins, continues to pursue, love, lead, and dwell within me despite all that I have done.

It's absolutely crazy forgiveness to not only cancel debts, but to go on as if no debt ever was owed, and I want in on that. I don't want to give a victim's statement, I decide. I want to reframe my story with a life statement putting God at the center of it all.

How to do so is my prayer as each day moves closer and closer to the moment I've anticipated for more than two-and-a-half years.

Here's How I Reframed My Story

At the last minute, Percy—perhaps swayed by the overwhelming DNA evidence against him—pleads guilty to all charges, and a court hearing scheduled for two weeks away is suddenly up in the air. So it comes as a surprise the morning of March 19, 2012 when my phone starts pinging with texts letting me know friends are praying for me. Come to find out, they had seen on the morning news the sentencing is to be 9 a.m.

Today.

It's a good thing I've been prayerfully preparing for a long time; I have no time to prep between when I find out from my friends' texts and when I rush into court. I barely have time to tell Sarah what I'm planning to say.

The nearly empty court room—so different from the arraignment, and the result of the last-minute time switch—is so quiet. The lone reporter and his camera crew fiddle with their equipment as I sit in the last row on a long wooded bench with only Sarah.

Then Percy is brought in, looking older and heavier. *He looks different every time I see him*, I think, my mind flipping from his burning eyes the night of the attack to his mean-looking mug shot to what I see before me. I can tell prison is hard on him.

Not long into the proceedings, Percy is made to acknowledge his guilt, one by one, to the four charges he is facing: larceny, first- degree home invasion, armed robbery, and assault with the intent to commit murder. Tension mounts when he hesitates at the judge's question as to how he pleads to the latter.

He is reconsidering his guilty plea.

"I never broke into his home with intentions of killing him," he says. "You are asking me to plead guilty to something I never did." It's a frustrating moment; I briefly wonder if I should give a victim's statement just so that Percy will fully understand he is not the victim himself.

"Sir," the judge responded, "you stabbed this man thirty-seven times. Which one of those thirty-seven stabs was not intended to kill him? It's by the grace of God this man is even alive today." Eventually, Percy reluctantly concedes.

With Percy's admission of guilt on all four charges, the bell rings for the final round in this fight to forgive.

Sarah is asked to go first. My wife, a champion among champions, has had so much to go through and deal with since the attack; she feels the court needs to hear the truth of how it affected our family. So without anger or ill intent, she simply begins sharing openly the suffering we've gone through, breaking down quickly in the process.

"His hands will never be the same; they'll never work the way he'd like, regardless of all the therapy we have been through," she tells the judge with tears streaming down her face. "His life will never be the same. Our kids' life will never be the same. I will never be the same because of what took place."

As I sit watching Sarah share, I am so proud of how honest she is. She is simply acknowledging the hurts, and by now I know full well how vital this is to moving forward. Listening to her makes it easier for me to follow her brave example; I may give sermons every Sunday, but I'm still a nervous public speaker. I know, though, what the Lord has called me to do; as I stand to my feet to make my way to the podium, four words return to my mind: "they still need you."

"Thank you for allowing me to speak," I start, gripping the podium as tightly as possible as my arms violently twitch out of extreme nervousness. "I know this is supposed to be a victim's statement, but today I refuse to give such a statement because I don't consider myself a victim. Instead, if you'd allow me, I'd like to give a life statement today and share what I've discovered, and some of the good that is coming about because of this attack.

"My life is forever changed in many ways. This man did break into my home. I have suffered pain and hurt because of what he did. Probably the biggest hurt I experienced is when I was lying on the floor about to die." My voice begins to crack. "I doubted where God was and that He abandoned me. It wasn't until after that I realized that when I felt God was the farthest from me, He had never been closer and more at work than He was than at that moment.

"Because of that night and what God has been able to bring me through, I've become a different person in so many positive ways. This may sound weird, but I am glad this happened because of the difference God has brought about in my life.

"Today I am a better father. I have different priorities in my life." It is in this moment, while beginning to share about being a parent, that I find myself beginning to turn to different individuals in the courtroom. For some reason, my eyes are led to the judge to begin with; I feel as if what I'm about to say is being shared between only the two of us.

"God has caused me to see how important my kids are and how much they need me. I have always loved them, but today it's different because I've made some changes to how I parent in light of what has taken place. I have made a decision to prioritize my involvement and presence in their lives. I've made a commitment that I will attend every event, even if it means walking away from work responsibilities."

Next I begin sharing about my marriage. Looking back and forth between the defense attorney to my left and the district attorney on my right, for some reason I feel these words are meant for them.

"Because of what God has brought me through, today I am a better husband. I love my wife and always have, but now I will never allow a day to go by where I am too busy, too upset, too distracted to tell her how much she means to me.

"Because of what God has brought me through, I am a better friend and a better son." Here, my mind flashes to one day when my mom, who was driving me to therapy, looked over at me and asked, "Have you ever been able to forgive me for leaving your dad?" I was shocked by the question; it had been nearly twenty years since they had divorced, and for many years I was bitter toward my mom. But that day, we talked about the past for the first time. Not only was I able to say I had forgiven her, I was able to ask my mom for forgiveness for being such an awful son to her. Our relationship was truly renewed in a matter of minutes, and all because God allowed wrongs and hurts in my life.

"Today I can also stand here and say I am a better pastor because of what God has allowed and brought me through. I see things differently than ever before." As I shared about pastoring, something inside of me was drawn to the reporter and the camera man who were recording every word. "For me, it has nothing to do with buildings, titles, being treated in a special way because I have a title—it's about people. I care about people in a way I never had because of what God has done in my life. My heart breaks for those who are hurting, and pastoring is no longer a job, a profession, a career; it is my life of loving and serving people."

Finally, I aim the very last of my life statement at the one responsible for what took place and the pain and suffering that followed.

"And lastly, I want to let Percy know that I have forgiven him completely. I am able to stand here today and forgive you because of how much the Lord has forgiven and continues to forgive me. Without the forgiveness of God, my life would be a disaster.

"I wish no ill will upon him whatsoever." I look toward Percy, who is to my side and a little in front of me; he continues to face straight forward. "If you ever want to make a change in your life for the good, I want you to know that I will be here and am willing to help you make that change if needed.

"I believe God has the ability to take Percy's life and bring good out of it. My prayer is that God would do exactly that—to do far more abundantly more than anyone could ever ask or imagine in him, because God is so good.

"Thank you for allowing me to share today." And with that, I walk back to my seat knowing that I have just delivered the knock-out punch in the fight to forgive the man who attacked me.

The fight started by revisiting the cross to rediscover how much I have been forgiven by God; the cross remains the place I return when tempted to be reoffended or hurt. Meanwhile, I conquered the spirit of fear by remembering that I belong to God, and by relying upon His Word and promises to fight for me when I become anxious. Bitterness had been uprooted through months and months of me daily praying for and blessing Percy, way before ever encountering him face-to-face. And with God's help, I've been able to prioritize serving others, thus preventing past wrongs and hurts from overtaking me in my race to love God and serve people.

Then, the decision I made way back in the hospital culminated in victory on March 19, 2012, when after more than two years of battling the Enemy's tactics, I was able to fully reframe my story. I am not Kevin Ramsby, pitiful stabbing victim who took a tennis racket to a knife and lost; I am Kevin Ramsby, stabbing survivor, overcomer, and servant of God, grateful to have been knocked off the treadmill of life and given the gift of change.

I meant every word I said in the courtroom that day, and I found that what brought me closure was having forgiven from the heart, as Jesus indicated we need to in Matthew 18:35. At that point, the prison sentence I'd obsessed about was simply the final step in legal procedures that issued consequences and justice. It was no longer something I needed in order to move on to years of God's greater good and purposes still on the horizon.

What a difference God makes when we make room for Him in our lives.

CHAMPIONS OF FORGIVENESS

Jesus and Joseph don't stand alone as winners in their own personal, challenging fights to forgive. The Bible is loaded with people who experienced great wrongs and hurts at the hands of others, yet trusted God and made it to the other side of forgiveness where God's intended purposes produced incredible and even heroic testimonies.

I call them the champions of forgiveness. Champions like:

- Moses, who forgave and served those who opposed his leadership (throughout Exodus and Numbers);

- David, who served King Saul faithfully even though the king was trying to kill him and make an enemy of him (see 1 Samuel 19-31);

- Hosea, who had to forgive a spouse who rejected and betrayed him (see Hosea 3);

- Eliam, Bathsheba's dad who (unlike his own dad Ahithophel) chose not to withdraw from David out of bitterness in the wake of the affair and loss of the baby that came out of it, but instead remained one of David's mighty warriors (see 2 Samuel 23);

- Mark, who could have written Paul off after Paul dismissed him from service in Acts 15:37-38, but instead took an open and forgiving enough stance for Paul to still consider him helpful and send for him later (see 2 Timothy 4:11).

But of all the Biblical champions of forgiveness, two men stand out in particular, as their stories so obviously involved tools I too discovered in the process of making room for God to turn intended evil into His greater good.

Stephen is one. Acts 7:60 shows that he returned to the cross for his fighting words when, in the midst of being stoned to death, he prayed for his attackers' forgiveness, just as Jesus had. As for the good that came out of it, Acts 8:1 mentions that Saul was among those who witnessed Stephen's victory in his fight to forgive. Saul actually approved of the killing at the time. But see, God always has the last word, and I don't think it is a coincidence that just one chapter after Stephen's heroic and Christ-like act of forgiveness, Saul is radically changed and becomes a forgiven man himself when he encounters the resurrected Lord on the Damascus road. Then Saul, once he became Paul, went on to write much of the New Testament. *That* seems like a pretty good example of God turning intended evil into His greater good, and I love how Stephen made room for it by winning his own fight to forgive.

Jephthah is the other Biblical champion of forgiveness who stands out to me; in fact, he has been even more of a role model in my journey of forgiveness toward God's greater good, as he actually followed a process just about identical to mine.

Judges 11 tells the story. After Jephthah was run off and denied his inheritance by his brothers for something over which he had no control—he was the result of their father's fling with a prostitute—

he lived as an outcast in a land where "a gang of scoundrels gathered around him and followed him." (Man, that sounds like me battling perspective, fear, bitterness, and flashbacks.) Still, he makes room for God to turn evils into His good when his offenders knock at the door in Judges 11:4 and he finds out that the Israelites are in trouble and his community needs him. In Judges 11:7, Jephthah quickly reveals the wrong (you're the ones who ran me off!) and acknowledges the hurt (he was a hated and outcast man). In Judges 11:9-11, he demonstrates trusting God, and by Judges 11:12, he is fighting for those who hurt him.

In other words, he doesn't stay trapped by the past, he quickly begins running from the lead—not because his wrongdoers made amends but because Jephthah adds God into the story. In doing so, he shows us that where he could have become bitter, he chose instead to forgive and make room for God to move in his life.

Then ultimately, he discovered his purpose. The Bible doesn't call Jephthah "the rejected prostitute's kid." God's Word calls him a mighty warrior.

I love that Jephthah's response to those who wronged and hurt him caught the attention of heaven so much that it even landed him in Hebrews 11, commonly known as God's Hall of Faith, where he is tucked in verse 32.

But you know, while I admire and look to these overcomers for guidance, I don't think God is done. In fact, I'm confident He still wants to finish some good works He has in mind, so He can add at least two more names to his Hall of Faith:

Mine. And yours.

PART FIVE

Discover God's Purposes

THE POWER OF FORGIVENESS

CHAPTER 32

"THEY STILL NEED YOU"

It's approaching seven years since the night of the attack as I write about my journey today, and I can report I am completely amazed at how forgiveness makes room for God to create new and exciting chapters for others—and even myself.

In the months following the trial, I reached out to Percy in prison to let him know my words there were genuine—that I would be there for him if he ever needed me. For the past several years, I've had the privilege of beginning to develop a cordial friendship with my former attacker, and I continue to pray for God to do a wonderful, transformational work in his life.

Meanwhile, remember God rescuing me with the words "they still need you"? I haven't forgotten that, and I'd love to share some of what has happened in that vein in the past six years.

One example began with sirens flashing in my rearview mirror. On the way to the church, cutting through neighborhoods, I had just rolled through a stop sign. Knowing I was busted with the church offices in plain view, I was really embarrassed as the officer made his way to my window.

"Hello, Pastor Kevin," the officer began, and I looked up to discover I'd been stopped by one of the first responders the night I was found on my neighbor's porch.

"Oh, hey there, Officer George. How's it going? I'm sorry, I totally know I didn't fully come to a complete stop back at that stop sign. I'm busted and I totally know it."

"Huh?" he replied. "Oh, I didn't see that"—and then I was kicking myself for opening my big mouth. "No. I recognized it was your truck and I just had to talk with you for a second."

It wasn't the first time I'd seen him since August 4, 2009; I'd first been reunited with him and his partner, the other first responder, months after the attack when we all responded to a 2 a.m. alarm at the church. I found out then—both from the shock on their faces (they looked like they were seeing a ghost) and in catching up— that the officers had had no idea I'd even survived. That night, they told me what they saw the night of the attack. How they felt. The adrenaline they'd experienced, having to go through my house, not sure if whoever did this to me was still inside. What it was like trying to keep me talking so I wouldn't lose consciousness. It had been an emotional, memorable reunion for all of us, and as time went on they would stop by the church every once in a while just to say hi and check on me. We'd formed an unbreakable bond.

"Pastor Kevin," Officer George began as I sat there holding my license and registration, "I pulled you over because I just had to let you know how much you have impacted my life. I've watched you return to the city. I've heard you share your story and everything you went through. And I've heard how you've chosen—and been able—to forgive the guy who nearly murdered you.

"I wanted to let you know that last week I went to church for the first time in a very, very long time. Your example really has inspired me, and God is working in my life. I just wanted to let you know because you really impacted my life."

I did *not* expect to discover that day how God was using what happened for His intended good.

"Wow. That is so awesome, Officer George," I told him. "It means the world to me that you'd pull me over to share this with me. That is so cool that you've begun attending church and God is working in your life. Is there anything I can do to help you on this new faith journey?"

There was, said my friend. "I went to church, but I don't have a Bible. Would you happen to have one?"

I smiled, thinking of the Bible bookstore the church owned. We headed there together, and it was one of my greatest honors to present a Bible, which has changed my life, to one of the officers who helped save it. When I reached out to Officer George recently to ask his permission to share this story, I learned he has been reading that Bible. It stays on his nightstand.

Officer George isn't the only one I've seen impacted by my fight to forgive. The wrongs and hurts I have experienced at the hands of Percy have turned out to be the very experiences in my life God needed to be able to bring hope and freedom to tens of thousands around the world as my story has been shared through "I Survived" (Discovery Channel), the 700 Club, Roma Downey's series "Answered Prayers" (TLC), Brooklyn Tabernacle's Easter Radio Program, and in writings by *New York Times* best-selling authors Mitch Albom and Pastor Mark Batterson. I've cried with fellow victims of violent home invasions, and

I've shed tears of hope and healing as rape victims, veterans dealing with post-traumatic stress disorder, betrayed spouses, and ministry leaders wounded while serving their church begin to engage in the fight to forgive their offenders.

It's been a privilege to go heart-to-heart with others in those encounters; frankly, that would be enough for me. In fact, after serving my beloved Revival Tabernacle through the transition from Pastor Tim's leadership and beyond, I resigned to begin working on this book to try to reach those who might need the message and tools God has given me in the wake of the attack. For all I knew, I might be getting a regular 9-to-5 job after that, just ministering to people one-on-one here and there. But God is "able to do immeasurably more than all we ask or imagine, according to his power that is at work within us" (Ephesians 3:20). In other words, He is not limited to my simple ideas, and what I discovered is His "immeasurably more" in my life is this:

He is not only calling me to continue pastoring in Detroit, He's calling me to a greater fight.

If that's a surprise to you, get in line. For a long time, I'd answer questions about whether my future holds pastoring with "most likely never again." In fact, at one low point in my struggles, I told Sarah I didn't have any more dreams. That is why I was completely surprised that after writing the parts "Revealing the Wrongs," "Acknowledging the Hurts," and "Trusting God," I began to experience a resurrection of a dream more than 20 years old. That is when the biggest part of the prize of winning the fight to forgive became apparent as I discovered, or really rediscovered, God's ultimate purpose for my life: planting a new church for the people of Detroit and beyond. When I could no longer contain this idea, I began sharing my thoughts with Sarah and a few people I've come to view as "Dream Encouragers" in my life; today, our dreams are more alive than ever as we prepare to serve and fight for the city and people we love.

So much for me and my limited goals. I'm thankful God always has the last say in my life.

And I believe He wants to have the last say in yours too.

CHAPTER 33

THEY STILL NEED YOU TOO

You intended to harm me, but God intended it for good. (Genesis 50:20)

Satan may have intended what Percy did that night to harm me, but I believe God intends good out of it that goes far beyond what He is doing with and through my life. Again, that's why I wrote this book: in case readers might find something useful in what I've been through. At the very least, I hope you can find hope in the fact that though I've struggled, I *have* been able to both forgive and discover God's purposes in my life.

But I think God has more to offer you than hope—a lot more, actually. I believe He hasn't forgotten the dreams still waiting to be fulfilled in your life, and I believe He not only wants to help and heal you, I believe He would love to help others through you as well.

In other words, there are people who still need *you* too.

So remember, though this fight begins with the wrongs and hurts produced by the actions of a person, the great news for you is that God ultimately has the last word and final authority in your life. You just have to make room for Him to turn their wrongs and your hurts into His greater purposes.

- Have you been wronged in life? Reveal that to others. That doesn't mean you have to write a book as I have, or address those who have hurt you the way Joseph and Jephtha did; it may mean being brutally honest with God, or sharing it with other people who have been hurt themselves. How you reveal it is much less important than making sure you do.

- Have you been wounded by people? Acknowledge that hurt. Don't pretend you can take a hit and keep on ticking when you're really letting things fester in darkness.

- Do you need to question a loving God who has allowed wrongs and hurts? Do it, and watch Him show you how to trust Him.

- Are you struggling with unforgiveness, fear, bitterness, memories, and being victimized by your past? Let it go by going to the cross, praying scriptures that combat fear, praying for those who hurt you, running from the lead by serving others, and reframing your story with God at the center and you as the victor, not victim.

- And finally, after conquering the opponents in your fight to forgive, get ready to discover God's greater good in you and greater works to be done through you.

Fair warning for those who step into the ring: This process starts out fairly easy but intensifies as it goes along. It's relatively easy to talk about who wronged you and what happened, and while some may bury hurts they have experienced, many are able to let the world know and see them without too much trouble. But trusting God gets a little more difficult, especially after He has allowed wrongs, and the road gets even rockier when you get to forgiveness. The truth is that some spend a lifetime exerting all their emotional energy telling, acknowledging and trying to trust, but never even getting into the ring of forgiveness that leads to the greatness God has for them.

But if you're up for the challenge, I believe you will make room for God to not only free you from the nightmares of your past but to reveal His purposes in *your* life. What could be more exciting than that?

One final thing: Please know it's a joy for me to try to help anyone who is hurting, particularly those who need help or encouragement in their own fight to forgive. Feel free to reach out to me by email at kevinramsby@yahoo.com.

May God bless and keep you.

Kevin Ramsby
kevinramsby@yahoo.com

Follow or support the ongoing ministry
of Kevin and Sarah Ramsby at
www.AFightToForgive.com

ACKNOWLEDGEMENTS

This project was far beyond my ability to create on my own. Thankfully, God surrounded me with an incredible dream team, especially my wife Sarah. Without your patience over these years and weathering the storms during my private battles, I would not be standing victorious. You have made me stronger, and you are the reason I continue to fight.

For their incredible personal support in allowing me to devote the time needed to write, I wish to thank Kevin and Debby Schiavo, Peter and Sandra Strek, Michael and Karen Moran, Dr. Renny and Rachel Abraham, Pastor Art and Shari Ledlie, Jim and Andrea Cockrum, Chris Kindred, Justin and Dr. Lynna Pillai, Chuck and Judy Weisner, and Kelvin and Kelly Squires.

Additionally, incredible people have played critical roles in our lives these past six years. A very special thank you to my mom, Nancy Harrington, who is the best mom and an even greater friend. You have taught me so much over these years, and I would not be the person I am without you.

Without love from the body of Christ and encouragement from certain pastors, I'm not quite sure how this story would have ended and what the next chapter of our life would look like. Thank you Pastor Tim and Cindy Dilena for navigating us through the most difficult year of our lives. Thank you to the gracious congregation of Revival Tabernacle for being there for us in so many ways and allowing us to serve you with so much brokenness still in our lives.

Thank you Pastor John Ortberg for taking time to speak to me, a complete stranger, and have one of the most meaningful conversations I've ever had. So much was at stake, and your encouragement right when I felt like quitting was a game-changer.

Sarah and I greatly appreciate Pastor Doug Combs and the Church on Fire congregation, who overwhelmed us with generosity at a critical point on our restoration journey and allowed us to rediscover the meaning of "home" again. Thank you to pastors Doug Schmidt (Woodside Bible), Jim Cymbala (Brooklyn Tabernacle), Wayne Murray (Grace Assembly of God), and Mark Batterson (National Community Church) for the incredible opportunities early on to share with your congregations and catch a glimpse in the eyes of your people of the need for this book and its message.

Thank you, Mitch Albom and S.A.Y. Detroit, for investing in and supporting some amazing Detroiters through Hope Village. Your generosity not only blessed others, it also empowered me to find victory over my past through serving those in our community who tend to be overlooked.

A special thanks to my editor Maureen Tisdale Batty, who handled this book with the care and openhandedness needed for me to trust anyone with it. You understood this was not just a project: it was, and is, my life. You believed in me and the good that could come out of sharing this often raw and emotional journey. Oftentimes, you believed in me and the purposes of this book more than I did myself, and for that, I am indebted.

Finally, I am most thankful to the Lord Jesus Christ. He has changed my life in every way. Not only did He rescue me from myself twenty-six years ago, but He rescued me from death and the hopelessness that ensued.